The Power of Process

By

Dr. Nikki Harris

DEDICATION

The Power of Process is dedicated to the people that walked me through this process and walked with me in this process. I want to dedicate this book to my husband, Apostle B. Donald Harris. Honey, you have been my greatest supporter, my prayer partner, my encourager, my friend, and foe (inside joke). Thank you, for making sure I never forgot who I was and the God that called me. Thank you, for never letting me give up on the dreams that God has placed inside of me. Thank you, for pushing when I wanted to stop and for walking through this process with me. Only you and the Lord knows what this process has been like. Thank you, for being patient with me as God has transformed me through this process. This has been a long, hard journey and you never gave up on me. I love you more now than ever! Clearly, God has been faithful!

To my Briana, I dedicate this book to you so you will know what it means to surrender to God completely, totally, and dangerously. Thank you, for being patient with mom as I have walked through this process. You literally grew up overnight, while I was writing this book. You were eight years old when I started this book and now you are a young woman. It is funny, we have kind of had our own process during *The Power of Process*. I love you and want you to know that God's way is always the best way.

To my Jeremiah, I dedicate this book to you so you will know the power in God's word and the power of His word. Writing this book was literally spiritual warfare. You were four when I started writing this book, now you are a teenager. I am encouraged that I taught you spiritual warfare as a result of this book. ***The Power of Process*** grew up with you as well. I dedicate this book to you so you will know, nothing with God happens by accident. Everything in our life is connected to our purpose. God does and allows everything on purpose. I want you to know and understand the power of prayer, fasting and the truth of God's Word that will propel you into destiny.

To Dominion Living Ministries, I dedicate this book to you. I want you to know it does not matter how long it takes, what you have to go through to do it, JUST DO IT! Give birth to every dream and vision God has placed in your heart and spirit. Thank you, for letting me practice with you. Thank you for being part of my team. The way I love you is indescribable.

CONTENTS

INTRODUCTION

Get Ready, Set, Wait! What?

So, you want to do "something great for God?" Have you had these questions pounding in your head, *Why am I here? What is it I am supposed to do?* Believe it or not, there is an answer. I am not talking about a one-stop shop to life's purpose. I am talking about the real pathway to true destiny. In my Christian journey, there has been a deep, passionate, burning desire to do something awesome for God. As I sat in churches, watched Christian television programs, listened to speakers and preachers, and read Christian books, I thought *I want to do that!* Unfortunately, when I heard them teach their process to destiny, I said within myself, "Yeah, I'm good God!" In my mind, I did a Bruce Lee back-up.

If you can walk with me on this journey, you will discover what I did. To do real work for God and to find your life's purpose, my friend, there is a process. Real estate gurus suggest one of the greatest keys to success is: location, location, location. Well, guess what? In the journey to purpose, destiny and eternal glory is process, process, process. "Get Ready, Set, Wait!" Yes, that is how God works. When we finally think we have it figured out, God determines to prepare us for our "wait". It is in our wait that we are processed for purpose. As I reflect, on what I have heard and experienced over the years, I have come to realize that people neglected to tell us about the process it took to get to where God has placed them. We must sound the alarm, so that others do not think they can microwave themselves into what God has planned for them. If we are honest, we all want the glory, but we do not want to live the story. Some of us wish we could be like Dorothy and click our heels together and—instantly—destiny! Sorry, my dear, it does not work like that. If people in the Bible went through trials, tribulations, beatings, scourgings and even death, unfortunately we must endure the same. Why? One of the immutable characteristics about God is that He does not change. God required much from all of them and He is requiring it of us, as well. Why have we convinced ourselves, that our pathway to purpose is like running through the morning dew barefoot? I have lived this message, while watching others avoid what I was going through, while others suffered the unthinkable. I want to invite you on a journey that will rip your heart in pieces, take your breath away, laugh you to tears and lead you into praise and thanksgiving for your journey. When you ask God for His will and aim to do it, buckle up, because it is going to be the most tumultuous, mind-bending, gut-wrenching, exhilarating ride ever! So here we go!

CHAPTER 1

THE PROCESS IS NECESSARY

"Don't Grow Weary"
Galatians 6:9

To understand the power that is unleashed through process, one must truly understand process. Process is a "series of actions or steps taken to achieve a particular end". In essence, process is the tools that are used to create, to perform or do a certain thing. Throughout the Bible, God used process to maneuver His divine will in the lives of His children. Some of His children welcomed the process, like Mary, and some struggled with the process, like Moses. Still others outright rejected the process, like Jonah. Their process was handcrafted by God. Honestly, we are no different from those we read about in the Bible. At times, we welcome the process, when we feel especially anointed and connected to the purpose of God for our lives. At other times, we behave like defiant toddlers when we cannot have our way, or when God's plans look nothing like ours. Process is exciting when we can discern its connection to purpose. Process becomes a horse of different color when we cannot see or choose not to see. When we cannot fathom the rationale behind the circumstances, situations, and occurrences in our lives, it can be difficult to welcome God's process. Sometimes, we get ticked off at God. If you are anything like me, you get tired of waiting and wondering about the "stuff" going in your life and want answers. Great news! God is not in Heaven playing chess with our lives, waiting to say, checkmate. He has a reason for the type of process, the length of the process and the outcome of the process.

Why Process?

Why does God use process to fashion us to His will? He is God, and He created everything. Seemingly, God would just tell us what He wants. And we would do it willingly, right? Nope, if that were so Adam and Eve would have never been kicked out of the Garden of Eden. God created us with the right to choose. It is our right to choose that makes the process necessary and worthwhile from Heaven's vantage point. God is a gentleman, he will not force us to do anything, although it can seem and feel like force. During my process, it has felt like force, but as I have walked through process, I learned the correct term is conforming.

So why process? Process helps shape us into the design that God intended when we were formed in our mother's womb. Unfortunately, life has a way of marring us into a person that is far from God's original design. We must be recreated and trained by our God through designed processes to fulfill purpose. Process from Heaven's vantage point is the picture of the potter and clay. If you have never seen how the potter forms his masterpiece, it is incredible. For me, it was a spiritual experience. The potter first decides what is to be created, then decides on the materials needed to create the masterpiece, the (masterpiece is silent during the creation phase), the potter then begins to fashion the masterpiece per the design he/she sees. The masterpiece transforms from imagination to reality. The masterpiece is designed without input from the finished product. The prophet Jeremiah eloquently depicts the process in Jeremiah 18:1-6, "The word which came to Jeremiah from the LORD, saying, Arise, and go down to the potter's house, and there I will cause thee to hear my words. Then I went down to the potter's house, and behold, he wrought a work on the wheels. And the vessel that he made of clay was marred in the hand of the potter: so he made it again another vessel, as seemed good to the potter to make it. Then the word of the LORD came to me, saying, O house of Israel, cannot I do with you as this potter? Saith the LORD. Behold, as the clay is in the potter's hand, so are ye in mine hand, O house of Israel."

We are born and shaped in iniquity; process conforms us into the image of Christ. The vicissitudes of life can mar us deeply. Everything has to undergo a process to become. For example, consider the wooden kitchen table in the most expensive furniture store. That table was once a living tree. The tree had to be ripped from the roots, dying as its source of life is being suffocated, while it is pulled from the Earth. It is sawed, cut, and fashioned into something usable for you and me. The beautiful family meals and memories made at our kitchen table would be impossible except that tree became a sacrifice for our memories. Sounds pretty graphic! Process often requires something in our life to be sacrificed to create something more beautiful.

Process is Beauty Wrapped in Pain

Pain and discomfort are vehicles our body uses to communicate that something needs attention. When pain becomes intensely uncomfortable, we listen and take the necessary precautions. Unfortunately, most of us must go through intense pain before we recognize that God needs to say something. Oh, how I wish, pain was avoidable, but it is necessary for real healing, deliverance, and transformation in our lives. Childbirth is the only identifiable act that I can think of to adequately depict beauty wrapped in pain. Before I had children, I was mortified by childbirth. Childbirth was described to me by my mother as, "Take your bottom lip, pull it over your head and staple it to a concrete ground". That sounds horrifying, but the beauty that comes from such excruciating pain in childbirth is indescribable. To behold the face of that beautiful baby, makes the pain seem insignificant…until you do it again!

Mary, the mother of Jesus, knew this kind of pain. She was not a stranger to incredible sacrifice for beauty to be born in her life. Her reputation was sacrificed for the life of the Savior. She appeared as a liar. Since when does a virgin, give birth? God was doing a new thing in the Earth. God sought to create an unforgettable moment. There was no way Mary could convince people that she was carrying the "holy child". She endured the pain of persecution to carry and birth Jesus. In the midst of pain, it can be hard to see the beauty.

God promises in Isaiah 61:3, "To appoint unto them that mourn in Zion, to give unto them beauty for ashes, the oil of joy for mourning, the garment of praise for the spirit of heaviness; that they might be called trees of righteousness, the planting of the LORD, that he might be glorified." Mary's pain brought the beauty of salvation into our lives. I am thankful Mary endured the pain of Jesus' birth and death, so that we can experience eternal life.

Queen Esther had to endure pain, but her pain brought her to the palace. It also brought deliverance for her people. Esther was orphaned and adopted by her uncle. Children who lose their parents feel incredible loss, hopelessness, and rejection. God must be allowed to heal from such deep-seated wounds. The death of her parents led her to her uncle, Mordecai putting her on the pathway to destiny. Esther's journey is the true fulfillment of Romans 8:28, "And we know that all things work together for good to them that love God, to them who are the called according to his purpose." Everything painful in Esther's life, God used it for her good and His glory. I should tell you that things are only made glorious when our vertical view is correct, and our hearts are fixed on the Lord. When we lose focus of God during pain, the beauty becomes marred and fragmented. Esther, a Jewish orphan girl became a queen, who was ultimately used for the deliverance of an entire nation. Her story has become a hallmark of God using the painful processes of death, loss, abandonment, and removal to a beautiful encore.

Process Positions for Purpose

In God's developmental lab, process is used to create, recreate, position, and reposition us for the fulfillment of God's will in our lives. Process is the "why" of a thing. Your process is often determined by God's plan for your life. When God desires a certain outcome for us; God uses certain circumstances, situations and occurrences fixed with the right amount of heat (pressure) that produces His desired purpose. In my own experience, certain circumstances with certain pressures produced certain outcomes. Without them, I would have missed the incredible imagery of God's handiwork in my life.

God has always used process in the lives of His children. We can see the examples in scripture. Most of His children yielded, while others decided to go their own way. Consider the life of Joseph, a prime example of God using process to position Joseph for his purpose and prophecy to be fulfilled in his life. Joseph was a dreamer, and God showed him that he would be a leader in and for his family. In Genesis 37: 5- 11, "And Joseph dreamed a dream, and he told it his brethren: and they hated him yet the more. And he said unto them, Hear, I pray you, this dream which I have dreamed: For, behold, we were binding sheaves in the field, and, lo, my sheaf arose, and stood upright; and, behold, your sheaves stood round about, and made obeisance to my sheaf. And his brethren said to him, Shalt thou indeed reign over us? Or shalt thou indeed have dominion over us? And they hated him yet the more for his dreams, and for his words. And he dreamed yet another dream, and told it his brethren, and said, Behold, I have dreamed a dream more; and, behold, the sun and the moon and the eleven stars made obeisance to me. And he told it to his father, and to his brethren: and his father rebuked him, and said unto him, what is this dream that thou hast dreamed? Shall I and thy mother and thy brethren indeed come to bow down ourselves to thee to the earth? And his brethren envied him; but his father observed the saying." Although, God had shown Joseph, the plan for his life, Joseph was not ready to walk in that purpose. Joseph needed to be developed. At the time of the dream, Joseph was immature and unable to handle the assignment. How he handled the dream was a strong indicator of his immaturity. Often God's process utensils bring spiritual maturity. The heat and pressure intertwined with circumstances and situations bends most of us into a posture of prayer. This posture is necessary for navigating the process.

God has used some very difficult circumstances that bent me into a posture of prayer that lead me directly to God's purpose for my life. As I walked through various process-oriented circumstances, I began to mature mentally, emotionally, and spiritually. I matured because of the process God was working in my life. People, things, and situations that would nearly drive me to insanity, pushed me to my knees. It drove me to a place of intimacy with God that I had never known. Many lives have collided with mine as a result of God walking me through process. Joseph endured some pretty ugly stuff; and all of it prepared him to be the prince of Egypt. Because he was sold into slavery, he ended up in Potiphar's house. While in Potiphar's house, Joseph had an encounter with Potiphar's wife. This led him to prison to interpret the dream of the cupbearer. The interpretation of the cupbearer's dream led him to Pharaoh. Joseph's encounter with Pharaoh positioned him to be present when the famine hit. Joseph's family had to come to Egypt for their survival and bowed before him and prophecy was fulfilled. Joseph's circumstances were tough and painful, yet they had divine purpose. Joseph learned not to despise the process because it was necessary for God's plan.

Despise Not the Process, Embrace It

In Christendom, we have such eloquent colloquialisms that sound great, but are hard to live. I admit, embracing the process that you are in can be difficult. I learned life is less complicated if you find reasons to rejoice. I was a chronic complainer, which made things harder, longer, and more painful. I was related to the children of Israel, who murmured and complained, as their eleven-day journey morphed into forty long years. When I finally got the message, I started to let my words be few and seasoned with grace. I applied mother wit, "If you can't say anything nice, don't say anything". This commitment did not change the circumstances immediately, but it changed me and my perception. Our perception can cause us to despise things.

We must see our life from Heaven's viewpoint. It can take some of the sting out of the pain, because we know that somehow God is going to allow good to come out of the hard places in our lives. To despise something means to feel contempt or deep repugnance. These are such strong words. I have felt contempt and deep repugnance for some of the things God has allowed to come visit and hangout in my life. So much so, that I shook my fists at God. Yes, I did. My life at times felt like a down-right curse. My perception was flawed. As I understood the process, God and His plan for my life, my process began to make sense. Instead of despising it, I began to embrace it. Experiencing rejection, pain, sickness, loss, abandonment, failure, death of loved ones and everything in between can make you feel like God is a liar. But the contrary is true, God is exactly who He proclaims to be, but your perspective must change to see Him.

Jesus, our ultimate example, demonstrated pure surrender and worship of the Father. Even Jesus, at the point of crucifixion, understanding his death was required for our eternal life. He prayed in the Garden of Gethsemane, "Saying, Father, if thou be willing, remove this cup from me: nevertheless, not my will, but thine, be done." Jesus embraced His process. Jesus recognized the cost and embraced it. As we journey through process, we will grow in maturity and be willing to surrender. Maturity in God ushers surrender more readily and eagerly. You cannot and will not embrace process, in immature faith. Which is why God allows process, it builds mature, rock-solid faith. It is this kind of faith that produces the miraculous. I realize that what God allows in my life, is more about me becoming like Him, maturing in Him, and yielding to Him.

My process has been necessary; without it I would not be who I am today, and you would not be reading this book. Maturing in God is needed, or we would be ever—learning, which is not a good thing (2 Timothy 3:7). Do not despise your process. There are truths about God and His word that are attached to it. Rejecting your process guarantees continual ignorance of the knowledge of God and His word.

The Process is Necessary

As parents, we know that certain things are necessary for our children to grow and mature. God is the world's best parent. He knows what is needed for our growth and development. Through process, we gain a better understanding of Him and His will. God owes us nothing... But His love makes it easy to approach Him.

For centuries, the church has created this fallacy, "You can't question God!" We have been lied to; we can question God. He expects us to question Him. If not, why does He tell us to come boldly before the throne of grace to find help in the time of trouble? Why does God tell us that if any man lack wisdom, let him ask God? Process gave me a correct understanding of God and His word. Process thrusted me to His arms, to my knees and prostrate on my face. This is so attractive to God. Our Father desires intimate connection with us. Process pushes us into intimacy with God, it has worked for centuries why would God stop now?!

God knew that Jonah's appointment in the belly of a whale would cause surrender, repentance, and obedience. God knew that Saul needed the Damascus road encounter because He would later need Paul. God knew a storm, would destroy Paul's ship and that Paul would be on broken pieces, which lead him to the island of

Melita because Publius and the people of Melita needed to be healed. The creative ingenuity of God knows exactly who He has created. We perpetrate as Inspector Gadget. We think we know what it will take for us to willingly obey God. We are clueless, this is why God is God. Hindsight is an incredible discerner. I have been able to read through my processes, who I am, where I am headed and why God has allowed some things. Like Jonah, I struggle with doing things God's way, exactly how He said do them. I am that child that sometimes needs a switch because I think I know more about my life than God. This is so prideful, I am ashamed. Many of us have secret pride that God is trying to deliver us from. Nothing exposes sin like process. God allows process to show us our little "ugly, deceitful hearts". God wants our hearts clean and pure. Process exposes, cleanses, bends, and points us into the direction of our Father's will. Process evokes the necessary prayer that brings about the necessary surrender, which brings about the necessary plan of God.

CHAPTER 2

PRAYING YOUR WAY THROUGH

"Pray continually*"*
1 Thessalonians 5:17

People are praying more now than ever. Unfortunately, people are praying about buying clothes and winning the lottery. We must learn how and what to pray to align with God and His will. To do that, we need to know what prayer is. Prayer is a solemn request for help or an expression of thanks to God. Prayer is spiritual communion with God. Now, that we understand what prayer is and who we should pray to, we can pray. We have been made to believe we need a degree in Bibleology to effectively communicate with God. If so, then we are in big trouble! Prayer is not screaming so loud that you burst the eardrums of your listeners. Nor do we have to pray so long that we fall into REM sleep, while listeners and onlookers hit the floor from exhaustion. Prayer is simply communicating and listening to God. We have to be careful that we do not become the cousins of the Pharisees and Sadducees. Experience has taught me that closet prayers are powerful enough to move mountains.

The Purpose of Prayer

To begin our prayer for purpose, we should know what purpose is. Purpose is the reason for which something exists, or is done, made, and used. Additionally, purpose is to set as an aim, intention, or goal for oneself. I have always wanted to know why I was born. I have found that this question is on the hearts of almost everyone. Okay, so now that we have a simplistic definition of purpose, how do we figure out what ours is? It is simple. We ask the One who made us. No, we do not need to have a conversation with our parents, although they had a huge part in our creation and may have some key information to help us. We must ask God. God tells us in Psalms 139:14, that we are "fearfully and wonderfully made".

Let us look at some basic things as we began to approach God concerning purpose. Has God ever told anyone what their purpose was? How did He tell them? What was their response? The answer to the first question is yes! In Jeremiah 1:1-7, God has a conversation with Jeremiah about his purpose. God tells Jeremiah that before he was formed in the womb, he was ordained a prophet! Wow! Before he was ever conceived, God had a specific purpose for his life. Thankfully, God does not show partiality, just as God had a purpose for Jeremiah, He does for us. In Jeremiah Chapter One, the Word of the Lord came to him, but Jeremiah did not directly pray. But Isaiah did. Remember prayer can be confession, too. Isaiah was repenting because of his condition and the fact that he could see God in His entire splendor. At the moment of Isaiah's confession, God clued Isaiah in on His purpose! God commissioned Isaiah to declare His Word, in Isaiah's place of brokenness. God has no partiality; we are not much different from the writers of the Bible. Both Jeremiah and Isaiah were told by God they had awesome purposes. They both responded like us, doubt, confusion, and fear. Both patriarchs were immediately aware of their imperfections, human fragility, and inability to complete the task. God called them anyway. God walked them through every step of their purpose because they relied on Him. God has a sense of humor because He called me! I am no Isaiah or Moses, but I have learned that as we walk out purpose, we can change churches, neighborhoods, cities and even nations!

Our Own Purposes

How do we utilize prayer to find our purposes? How do we ensure that what we think "our purpose is" has really been God-breathed? We have this innate desire to do what we want, when we want, and how we want. Unfortunately, this is in direct opposition to the plan of God. Often, we desire "purposes" that are outside of the will of God. So then, how will you and I know if our purpose is aligned to the will of God? Ask God. I know you were expecting an exuberant theological anecdote, but no. Purpose is found by asking God through prayer. We may not experience altar utensils touching our tongues or bushes burning in a distance. And we probably will not have a prophet to pour oil on us in front of our siblings. But God, will instruct and lead us if we are willing to endure the process! The process God takes us through will conform our character to His. As we pray through our purpose, we should see the ungodliness in our character being chiseled away. Prayer has always been used to talk to God. Prayer is a discipline you must practice to be effective. Believe it or not, the more we pray, the more we will discern God's voice. We learn God's voice through prayer and His word. So how do you pray?

How will you know that your prayers are heard? There is no specific formula that I can dictate, nor am I going to recommend reading a prolific dissertation on the rules for praying. God answers the smallest, seemingly insignificant prayers.

The Purpose of God

God really appreciated the hearts of those that sought Him individually. I really love the relationship that Moses and Abraham had with God. Their relationship with God depicts how God can speak purpose through prayer. Their lives convey real two-way conversation with God. Many theologians consider Abraham to be the father of faith. He believed in a God that he did not know. In Genesis Chapter 12, we see the call of Abram, his journey communing with God and discerning God's purpose for him. The life of Abram began with God speaking directly to him, The LORD had said to Abram in Genesis 12:1, "Go from your country, your people, and your father's household to the land I will show you." Wow! How awesome is this! The God of Heaven tells you exactly what to do! God still does this, but the problem is many do not know God is talking. Hence, the needed discipline of prayer and studying the Word of God. God told Abram what to do and how his obedience would be rewarded, "I will make you into a great nation, and I will bless you; I will make your name great and you will be a blessing. I will bless those who bless you, and whoever curses you I will curse; and all peoples on earth will be blessed through you (Genesis 12:2-3)." God spoke to Abram, gave instructions, and promised positive end results! Notice, I said *end results.* If we continue to study the life of Abram, whose name was changed to Abraham, we will see a man developing a relationship with His God. His relationship included regular communion, fellowship, and hearing God's voice. We also see the "process" that Abraham went through to obtain the promises of God. We know that Abraham's purpose was to be a "father of many nations". But his wife was barren. This purpose required God. The purpose God has for us requires God. In Genesis Chapter 18, God speaks to Abraham concerning His will and let Abraham know He is preparing to destroy the city. Abraham pleads with God to spare the righteous. Abraham pleaded with God (prayed) about the righteous in the city and God responds to Abraham's requests. This encounter shows us two things: (1) God wants us to know His will (2) God wants us to play an active part in His will in our lives and the lives of others. There is such power in the prayers that we pray to God.

Let us go back to the question of "How do we pray?" As we look at the life of Abraham, we do not see Abraham on his knees, lying on the floor prostrate, we see Abraham talking to God. There are many postures of prayer throughout the Bible. The important side note: people prayed. The people talked to God. You pray by talking to God. God responds to the sincere heart of the person praying. Growing up, I often heard God does not hear a sinner's prayer. If he does not, then how does one get saved? Our communication with God should be aligned with the Word of God. The alleviation of prayer only makes the process more difficult.

Purpose in Persecution and Pain

The life of Moses is picturesque of our lives. Many of us, like Moses, were born in places where our life-expectancy was decided by our circumstances. Moses was born when all male children were to be killed. In first chapter of Exodus, a new king arose

(Pharaoh), but was not familiar with Joseph and his connection with the children of Israel. Pharaoh saw no reason to show them kindness. Pharaoh believed that the children of Israel were a threat. Isn't it amazing that the enemy saw their worth even in their bondage? Wow! Pharaoh purposed in his heart that the best decision was to set taskmasters (oppression) over them and burden them with slavery to build more cities. Ironically, the more the children of Israel were oppressed, the more they grew. Satan still uses this strategy. He has not learned that the more he afflicts a child of God, the more they will pray and the closer they will get to the will of God. Pharaoh instructed all the midwives of the Hebrews to watch all the births. All the girls had life granted to them, but the boys were to be killed. Pharaoh decreed death but God declared "deliverance."

Moses' parents could not rejoice about his birth. When we are born in destitute places of pain, agony, and hardship, we think it hinders our purpose. The circumstances you are born into are connected to your purpose. Moses was called to be "the deliverer", yet he made some terrible mistakes on his journey. This deliverer committed murder. Wow! Most would think this would forfeit his purpose. It did not; it brought him closer. Please, do not misunderstand me. In no way, am I advocating murder. Murder is sin and sin without repentance is death in the sight of God! After Moses killed the Egyptian, he fled to Midian where he met his appointment with the burning bush. If this dreadful mistake by Moses did not cost him his destiny, then you and I still have a chance.

The Call of Moses

We must engage in continual communication with God. In Exodus Chapter Three, Moses begins his communication with God. The burning bush burned from a distance and got Moses' attention. God does not change; he still uses different things to draw our attention to Him. Moses recognized the burning bush and then God calls his name. Moses responds with the answer that God desires from all of us, "Here am I". Moses responded correctly even before he knew what was expected of him. Most of us want God to tell us first and then we will respond. God does not work that way. Oh, how I have wished He did! Notice what God does, he tells Moses who He is, why He is present and what He requires. In Exodus 3:11, Moses responds like most of us "Who am I that I should go unto Pharaoh and bring forth the children of Israel out of Egypt?" I am sure I am not the only one that said, "Who me?" God does not address Moses's fears. God says in Exodus 3: 12, "And God said, "I will be with you. And this will be the sign to you that it is I who have sent you: When you have brought the people out of Egypt, you will worship God on this mountain." God is so awesome. God sees the end result. God sometimes allows the pathway to destiny to be difficult so that you and everyone else will know He is God.

The Equipping of Moses

Moses continued to talk with God; Moses begins his process of taking God at His word. In Exodus Chapter Four, God equips Moses. God always equips us for our assignment and God uses process as a strategy. To survive the process, we must pray; the process can get pretty scary! In the same chapter, Moses reminds

God that the people will not hear him, after God already told him that he would deliver them. God trained Moses to trust Him. God and Moses continue to dialog about Moses' feelings of inadequacy. In Exodus 4:3, God asks Moses *"What is that in your hand?"* Moses responds, "A staff." God instructs Moses to throw the staff down and it becomes a snake. And Moses ran. To all those people, who said you were supposed to be like Hercules, tell them Moses was scared. Yet, He delivered the children of Israel out of Egypt. In our process, sometimes the situation will be scary, but it is designed to build faith and trust in God. Moses was overly concerned about the inadequacy of his speech. God likes to use us in uncomfortable places! Get comfortable being uncomfortable. Moses was so concerned about his speech; he pleads with God. God humors him by allowing his brother Aaron to go with him. Moses still did all the talking. Moses is a great example of responding in obedience despite our feelings and inadequacies. It is the continual prayer to God that makes the difference. When the storms get tumultuous, the tests get scary, and the enemy gets stronger, prayer is the vehicle through.

CHAPTER 3

A FAST IS REQUIRED

"But when you fast, put oil on your head and wash your face."
Matthew 6:17

A Fasting Perspective

Fasting is vital to our Christian walk. It is paramount to discerning our purpose. It can be difficult to discern purpose if we cannot clearly hear God. We have looked at Abraham and Moses, let us look within. We have difficulty hearing God because we do not recognize His voice. We do not know His word. God will not speak outside of His Word. My husband is a pastor, many times while preaching he mentions that God gives a rhema word wrapped inside the logos word. Let me explain. A rhema word is often defined as the "spoken word of God" and the logos word is often defined as the "written word of God". In layman's terms, the rhema word is "that word" given to a person that is saturated in the logos word (the Bible). This is important because during fasting, God usually gives us "that word" to move us forward in our purpose. Fasting is a very real part of my life. I was taught to fast, so I know the importance of fasting. When my world flipped upside down, I needed some answers. The best way to get those answers was to get in the face of the Almighty God! God was requiring things of me, which made no sense to me. I would have never obeyed God without fasting. I needed clarity, I had to "push my plate aside" as the old saints called it. Fasting requires a level of discipline that is only learned through practice. God is gracious, He tells us what steps we can take to help us find our purpose. In Matthew 6:17, "But when you fast, put oil on your head and wash your face", Jesus is instructing the disciples on fasting and what the end result is if they follow his instructions. Now, if the disciples were given instructions to fast, and Jesus fasted, why do we think we can bypass fasting? So, in case you thought fasting was not necessary, think again. People have gotten so cute with fasting now. We have found so many different types of fasts and I wonder did any of these come out of the Bible. In an effort to be deep, we have missed the reasons for fasting and forfeited the benefits.

Biblical Fasting

There were many who fasted for spiritual purposes. Fasting has been designed by God to bring closer communion with Him, as well as physical and natural blessing. Fasting is not as easy as it sounds. Why? Fasting is designed for spiritual purposes and spiritual purposes have spiritual instructions that can only come from a Spiritual God. Fasting gets God's attention in ways that prayer cannot do alone! Fasting must be defined according to scripture. Fasting is the abstention of food, water, both, and certain types of food for spiritual purposes (Isaiah 58:1-7; Daniel 1:12; Matthew 4:2; 1 Kings 19:6-8; Esther 4:16). Before we discuss the different types of Biblical fasts, we must understand what the Bible says about fasting. The Bible gives clear instructions on fasting and the results of fasting (Isaiah 58:1-14). I should tell you that fasting should not be used to lose weight (sorry, but true!).

Fasting has a spiritual connotation if you desire the spiritual results.

There are two important factors to consider when determining if your fast meets Biblical qualifications. In Isaiah 58, the prophet Isaiah was commissioned by God to remind the people that their fasting was not recognized by God because their hearts were not in the right place. It should be understood that in order to get what you need from God through fasting you should align your heart to God and the fast is then in biblical order. Second, the fast must be chosen by God, in other words does your fasting fit the requirements of scripture. Are you fasting to humble yourself? Are you fasting for someone to be loosed from the chains of injustice (deliverance)? To untie the cords of the yoke of bondage (concerns or matters of the heart)? Let the oppressed go free (salvation)? And that ye break every yoke (revelation of the strategy of the enemy)? If the reason you are fasting does not fall into one or more of these categories, you might want to reconsider your motive! Many of the Bible patriarchs fasted for various reasons. They got amazing results. The fast of Moses, Elijah, and Jesus had very distinct ministry purposes attached. Often, people seek to be "Spiritually Deep", and attempt an absolute forty-day fast. Unless you are Moses about to deliver the Ten Commandments, Elijah who shut up the heavens and annihilated wicked prophets, or Jesus, that fast is not for you.

The Daniel Fast

Today, The Daniel Fast is the most adopted fast in Christendom. With that said, we will discuss the Daniel fast. The Daniel fast, is more easily embraced than a liquid or absolute fast. The Daniel fast has been publicized in books, television programs,

even some non- Christians utilize this fast. Lacking understanding in the power of a Daniel fast, can cause one to take it lightly.
What we call the Daniel fast, was Daniel's determination to obey
God at all cost, even death. Daniel made a decree that he and his
friends would fare better than those who partook of the king's
meat. In Daniel Chapter One, Jehokiahim, king of Judah requested
that certain children of Israel be selected with certain abilities.
These abilities included no blemishes, well-favored, skillful in all
wisdom, cunning in knowledge, and understanding in science and
had the ability to stand (blend-in) in the king's palace. Daniel met
the qualifications that the king requested; he did so because of his
firm commitment to the Lord. All of the children that were selected, were given a daily portion of the king's meat and the king's
wine. These selected vessels had to do this for three years before
they could stand before the king. Daniel and his friends: Meshach,
Shadrach, and Abednego refused to partake in the eating of the
king's meat and the drinking of the king's wine. In verse 12, Daniel purposed in his heart that he would not defile himself with the
portion of the king's meat, nor the wine which he drank; therefore
he requested of the prince of the eunuchs that he might not defile
himself.

Typically, the refusal to obey the king resulted in death. But
Daniel had favor with God and that favor was extended to the
prince of the eunuchs. In Daniel 1:10, the prince of the eunuchs
talked with Daniel about the eating arrangement that he was
suggesting. He informed Daniel that he and his friends were going to look sickly if they did not conform to the king's request.
Daniel knew that if he obeyed God and adopted His principles
there was no way he could lose. Therefore, Daniel made a proposition to the eunuchs. The proposition was that he and his friends

be allowed to eat only pulse (fruit and vegetables) and drink water for ten days and prove that their countenance would be better than those who partook of the king's food. This is the first recorded fast that Daniel and his friends embarked upon. In Daniel 1:15, the Bible records that at the end of ten days their countenances appeared fairer and fatter in flesh than all the children which did eat the portion of the king's meat. As a result, the prince of the eunuchs took away the king's meat from the others and gave them what Daniel and his friends had eaten.

Daniel witnessed the power of God to a wicked king and his servants. Daniel and his friends benefited from this fast. They received knowledge and skill from God and Daniel was given the prophetic ability to interpret dreams. How awesome is it to stand on God's principles and watch God back you up! Daniel and his friends were more favorable than all that were in the kingdom. I am sure if Daniel had not fasted, he would not have known the breadth of his prophetic ability. His prophetic ability brought him before great men. In Proverbs 18:16, "A gift gets attention; it buys the attention of eminent people (*Message Bible*). As with Daniel, if we fast God can unlock some of the hidden gifts in us. These gifts can bring us before great men who may have access to the keys, we need to unlock our destiny.

Esther's Absolute Fast

Esther and the Jewish people went on a three-day absolute fast (no food and no water) for deliverance. In Esther Chapter Four, Mordecai begin to weep before the gate concerning the decree that was sent out by Haman to annihilate the Jews. Esther's handmaidens and chamberlain learned of Mordecai's weeping and told it to Esther. As a result, Esther became very grieved and sought clarification. Mordecai requested that Esther go before the king on their behalf. Esther sent word to Mordecai that going before the king unannounced could cost her life and that she could not appear before the king for another thirty days. Mordecai reminded Esther not to think of herself, and reminded her that if she did nothing, her entire race would be destroyed. Mordecai asked her one question, "And who knoweth whether thou art come to the kingdom for such a time as this?" What if your purpose is linked to the deliverance of an entire generation? You may never know that if you do not fast and pray.

In Esther 4:16, Esther sent word to Mordecai, to gather all Jews that were present in Shushan, and fast. She asked them not to eat or drink anything for three days. This fast was necessary to ensure that the presence of God accompanied Esther as she approached the king unannounced. Unannounced visits to the king meant death. Esther purposed in her heart that she would avenge her people from death. God intervened on behalf of Esther and her life was spared. The miracle was that the king promised to grant Esther whatever request she presented to him. God exonerated the Jews and Mordecai was Haman's replacement. This fast gave Esther the grace and courage to risk her life for the deliverance of her people. Esther's fast guaranteed divine protection and ultimate victory over the plot of the enemy.

Moses' Fast

In Exodus 34:28, "Moses was there with the LORD forty days and forty nights without eating bread or drinking water. And he wrote on the tablets the words of the covenant—the Ten Commandments." This is the indication that Moses fasted for forty days and forty nights. I am sure it was not difficult to fast because he was in the presence of the Almighty God. Moses had been given the task to write the Ten Commandments on the second tables of stone. Moses gave God's law to the children of Israel and this was a one-time assignment.

The knowledge of the Bible helps us to clearly discern fasting properly. Just in case, you think God has called you to this kind of fast you may want to check the voice you are hearing with the Word of God. 1 John 4:1, declares, "Dear friends, do not believe every spirit, but test the spirits to see whether they are from God, because many false prophets have gone out into the world." This scripture suggests that we try every spirit by the Word of God. If you study the Word, you will see each person that endured a forty-day fast had a specific assignment, for a specific moment in time, and there are no more candidates for these specific assignments.

Elijah's Fast

Elijah's fast is depicted in 1 Kings 19:5-8. Elijah traveled forty days and forty nights on one meal, until he reached Horeb, the mountain of God. If you continue to read the story of Elijah, you will find that Elijah had the responsibility of anointing Hazael to be the king of Syria, anointing Jehu to be the king of Israel and anointing Elisha as a prophet. In Biblical times, if you had the responsibility to appoint or anoint someone to their God-appointed position and you incorrectly applied the anointing it could mean the destruction of a kingdom. This absolute forty-day fast helped Elijah to correctly apply the Word of God to the right person and set the will of God in order for two nations.

Our Savior's Fast

Jesus' fast is reflected in the four gospels: Matthew, Mark, Luke, and John. In Luke 4:1-2, the Bible states, "And Jesus being full of the Holy Ghost returned from Jordan, and was led by the Spirit into the wilderness, being forty days tempted of the devil. And in those days, he did eat nothing: and when they were ended, he afterward hungered." Most understand this was the beginning of Jesus' ministry. Jesus was tempted by the devil before he began his public ministry. Jesus was full of the Holy Ghost and he was the Word made flesh. The ministry fulfilled by Jesus could only be done by Jesus. His fast set us free.

Personal Experiences with Fasting

Have you ever had such a busy day that you forgot to eat and did not feel hungry? Well, in my personal experience with fasting, when I have set my mind to fast, my stomach growls so loud that it sounds like a thunderstorm! But the day before when I forgot to eat no problem! I wonder why? Fasting is for spiritual purposes. Every time, I set my mind to fast, everyone wants to take me to lunch, dinner and my favorite doughnuts are on sale at Wal-Mart! I have to pray really hard to stay focused! I quote, "The Spirit is willing, but the flesh is weak (Matthew 26:41) like my life is hanging in the balance.

I am almost embarrassed to write this, I used to have food mares! A food mare is a nightmare, where I am binging on food or being attacked by food! Can you believe that? After day three, I would conquer and annihilate the killer hamburgers, chicken, and pizzas. We must discipline ourselves and fast. I grew up in a Christian home, I learned to fast early. I did not understand the value of fasting until I became a young adult building a relationship with God. The very first time I fasted for a spiritual purpose concerning my life, I was a sophomore in college. I was a biology/pre-med major and school was taking a huge bite out of me! I was so stressed, losing weight, my hair was shedding, and chemistry was standing in my chest on top of my heart. Chemistry said, "I am going to kill you before this semester ends!" Imagine the horror!

I remember calling my mother in tears, after I barely passed another chemistry test. She listened and then told me of a dream she had about me. She told me to pray, seek God and discern if being a medical doctor was God's will for my life. What she believed the Lord had for my life and what God revealed to me, was not what I had in mind! I honored my mother and began seeking the Lord through prayer and fasting. I began a seven-day journey of prayer and fasting. Each morning, I anointed my head with oil as described in Matthew 6:17 and prayed every chance I got. I prayed between classes and work, trusting God would clue me in on His will. During the fast, God began to reveal His purposes and plans for me concerning my education and career. His will was very different from mine. Not only did God clue me in, but he also confirmed Himself in all of my uncertainty. The funny part is my conversation with God was about how much money I would not be making if I obeyed what He was saying. To a twenty–year old, big money, power and prestige was the reason for going to college. I needed to be important and rich. I went to school to become a cardiovascular surgeon; the hilarious part is that seeing blood and guts made me nauseous! But a salary with a bunch of zeros, would be worth the days of vomit, in my mind.

God's plan was for me to be a teacher. A teacher! Are you kidding me? I did not even like children enough to be with them all day! Teachers made nothing in comparison to a cardio-vascular surgeon! Geez, I wanted to know if God was sure that He was talking to the right person. I was raised in a Christian home and after spending ridiculously long hours in church, I managed to hear a story about Gideon. I heard the story of Gideon at one of those services when I was paying attention and not thinking to myself "How much longer? People please!" So, with my twenty-year old intellect, I applied Gideon's principles to my current situation. To my surprise, God responded as I had asked. I asked the Lord to allow a stranger to confirm what He was saying. The day after I prayed this prayer, I traveled home for the weekend with my friend, we will call her Cindy. On the drive home from school, I shared my concerns and asked her to be praying with me about it. Well, we stopped by her home, before I went home. I had never met her parents, particularly her stepmom. Cindy had gone to put her things down. As she was walking back to the dining room, where her stepmother and I were sitting and talking, the scariest thing happened to me. Her step-mother looked directly in my face and said, "Have you ever-thought about being a teacher? You should really pray about this. I was dumbfounded and I looked directly at Cindy and she had the same look on her face as I did. There was no way she could have known this. We did not have any contact with home while we were driving. Neither of us had cellphones; we were not doctors. I was totally blown away! God had answered my prayer and honored my fast very quickly. I was getting nervous!

I was new at this 'taking God at his Word thing" and like Gideon, I got even more detailed and specific with my request.

Again, God responded as I had asked. When I got back to school that Monday, I prayed and asked God to show me where to go and who to talk to. When I finished praying, the Lord instructed me to go to Gooch hall, I had no idea where the building was. You would think I would pick up a phone and find out. But I was still trying this thing out, I was instructed to go out of my dorm room, take a left, keep straight, and then make a right. I followed those instructions and to my surprise it landed me in front of Gooch hall. Wow! I had passed that building so many times. I went into the building went to the elementary office and changed my major to elementary education.

In obedience, I surrendered my desire to be a rich hot-shot surgeon to the lowliness of an elementary school teacher. When I changed my major, I went from barely passing courses to being on the dean's list until I graduated from college. I believe I have saved more lives as an educator than I ever could as a surgeon and without the blood and guts! Gideon's principles have been lifesaving and I have used them multiple times. For those gut-wrenching, soul-searing and life–altering decisions, I fast when needed. I believe God intervenes in my life because I fast regularly. Fasting works, I will never forsake this discipline.

Nehemiah's Fast and Results

The prophet Nehemiah's fast caused major change in his nation and with his people. Nehemiah was given a burden by the Lord (or purpose) for the Jews and Jerusalem. He prayed and fasted for them and God gave Nehemiah instructions on how to work in concert with Him. In Nehemiah Chapter One, Nehemiah has a conversation with one of his brethren Hanani, who discloses the fate of the Jews and Jerusalem. When Nehemiah hears this travesty, he is burdened. We know he is burdened because the Bible records in Nehemiah 1:4, "And it came to pass, when I heard these words, that I sat down and wept, and mourned certain days, and fasted, and prayed before the God of Heaven." Let me provide a little insight regarding burdens. A burden means "that which is carried; load; that which is borne with difficulty." The word burden in Greek is *forteon* which means load or of the obligations Christ lays upon His followers. This is important because sometimes our purposes are directly linked to a burden that God places on our hearts like Nehemiah. Many have accomplished mighty things because a burden was placed on their heart by the Lord.

Nehemiah's Burden of the Lord

Nehemiah's heavy burden ushered him into a period of prayer and fasting for four months. God gave him insight on three things: his purpose, the affliction and captivity of the Jews and the broken-down wall of Jerusalem. Before Nehemiah closes his prayer to God, he requests that God grant him mercy in the sight of King Artaxerxes. Nehemiah was the cupbearer of the king. Nehemiah knew that the king could assist him in completing his purpose. Nehemiah requested that God give him favor to accomplish this task, God did. God will always give us the spiritual grace and guidance to accomplish whatever task He assigns to our hands.

Following God's Agenda

God will often supernaturally orchestrate meetings for us. These meetings usually play a vital role in the fulfillment of our purpose. God even uses the places where He has planted us to bring forth our purpose as well. Notice, Nehemiah was already in the king's palace and the king had the ability to furnish what Nehemiah needed to get to Jerusalem. Nehemiah was so heavily burdened, that the king noticed and inquired of Nehemiah's burden. Nehemiah shared his burden with the king. And the king asked Nehemiah if he could help. In Nehemiah 2:4, "The king said unto me, for what dost thou make request? So, I prayed to the God of Heaven." Nehemiah had spent four months before God. God instructed Nehemiah on how to respond to the king. Nehemiah made his request to the king and he obliged. When God has a planned purpose for your life there will be favor and mercy to accomplish the task. Provision will be available as it is needed. Favor and mercy do not mean easy or swiftness to accomplish the task. If you continue to read the story of Nehemiah, you will see the obstacles he faced. But you also see the favor and grace to accomplish the rebuilding of the wall of Jerusalem. We must understand that God allows or creates obstacles so that we will know it is all Him. These obstacles birth greater faith in God.

The king gave Nehemiah the letters he needed for his travels and he provided protection. Here, we see God manifesting for Nehemiah as Jehovah Jireh. "Jehovah" means God or (YAWH) and Jireh meaning "The Lord Will Provide." God will always provide answers and provisions for those who seek Him through fasting and prayer. Nehemiah's purpose was to rebuild the wall of Jerusalem, which he did in fifty-two days. God anointed him to build because building contractors are slow as turtles. Nehemiah learned his purpose through fasting and prayer. Nehemiah lived a life of prayer and fasting and accomplished much for God. Fasting can yield generational returns and rewards.

Silence is Golden

My mother used to say, "silence is golden." Silence when operating in the realm of God is necessary for your effectiveness. Nehemiah was brilliant, he arrived in Jerusalem silently. Sometimes, we must keep silent until God gives the appointed time of revelation. We will encounter enough obstacles without the intrusion of other opinions. In Nehemiah 2:12, Nehemiah discloses his actions, "And I arose in the night, I and some few men with me; neither told I any man what my God had put in my heart to do at Jerusalem; neither was there any beast with me, save the beast that I rode upon." Nehemiah's one act of intense prayer and fasting had remarkable impacts. Can you imagine the level of impact our lives would have if we regularly engaged in prayer and fasting? Nehemiah's fasting not only prepared him for the task, but to face and conquer the obstacles he encountered.

Working Through the Hindrance

In Nehemiah Chapter Six, Sanballat was not happy about Nehemiah's accomplishment and started a rumor that Nehemiah and the Jews intended to rebel. Sanballat contended they were rebuilding the wall so Nehemiah could be king. Sanballat and others conspired against Nehemiah, to hinder his work. Nehemiah's response to the conspiracy was prayer and he and his team continued working. Their diligence angered the conspirers even more. They were so angered because Nehemiah ignored them, and they sought to go to war with Nehemiah. Nehemiah continued to work despite the obstacles. As God reveals your purpose, and you commit to fast for direction and discernment, there will be natural and supernatural conspirers strategically designed to hinder your purpose. As the opposition arises, gain clarity from God, and then proceed amid the opposition. *Fasting bulldozes the barriers that stand between you and the answer from God!*

My Burden of the Lord

God placed a purpose- driven burden on my heart. A unique part of my purpose is to minister to ministry wives. This burden was placed on my heart three years after I married my minister-husband. My level of understanding was not where it is now. I was a young wife, I had difficulty discerning purpose of this magnitude and I definitely did not understand what it meant to have a "burden from the Lord". All I remember is just being so empty inside and desiring more knowledge about how to be my husband's wife. I had other friends who were married, but none at the time were married to ministers. The stuff I went through they did not understand. I was not close enough to my pastor's wife to be that transparent. I longed for camaraderie with someone who could identify with me. During this season, I read books written by ministry wives, I read articles and magazines. I read anything I could get my hands on to help me. Two years after my husband started pastoring, I began to understand why God had allowed me to feel the things I felt, experience the things I experienced, and encounter the people I encountered.

God was birthing "By His Side Ministries", into my life. By His Side Ministries, is a ministry that addresses the needs of ministry wives. It is unique in that it does not exclude ministers' wives. Most ministries for women married to a man in ministry are just for the pastor's wife. I was a minister's wife for so many years before my husband was called to pastor. I needed support, encouragement, and impartation. I dare not leave a minister's wife behind. In 2008, God began to burden me about this ministry, the purpose and how to carry it out. Unfortunately, I was too busy being "educator extraordinaire" and had little time for my "real purpose".

The Power of Fasting

There are many examples in the Bible of the power of fasting. Mark 9:29 records, "And he said unto to them, this kind can come forth by nothing, but prayer and fasting". Some things only happen through prayer and fasting. Yes, that means certain things God will only reveal when you fast. It is possible that you may not know your purpose because you have not yet fasted. Fasting is a discipline that requires some muscle strength, spiritual muscle strength that is. Fasting sharpens your ability to hear the voice of God and it empowers you to do the will of God.

If you have never fasted before let me encourage you to embark on a fasting journey. Your stomach might try to bite you, your mind may try to talk you out of it and your will may get the best of you. If you fast, you will have an exhilarating experience with God! As the old saints would say, "It is time to push the plate aside, and hear what God's got to say about it!" There are answers to prayers and purpose awaiting on the other side of the fast.

CHAPTER 4

❦

PURIFYING PREPARATION

*"Those who cleanse themselves from the latter will be instruments
for special purposes, made holy, useful to the Master and
prepared to do any good work."*
2 Timothy 2:21

Purification Defined

The last thing you want to hear about is purification. We
have already talked about praying without ceasing and fasting regularly. Practicing these two disciplines on a regular basis
is an automatic catalyst for purification. When I think of purification, I think of cleansing. I picture Brita-water, a water filtration
system that is placed over the faucet for cleaner, healthier, and
purer water. We like our water, food, and clothes clean. God
wants us spiritually clean. Purification is the act of cleaning and
getting rid of impurities. God wants us to rid ourselves of impurities before catapulting us into purpose. Uncleanliness can hinder
your ability to hear God, prolonging, and impeding purpose.
What we think our purpose is, and the actuality of our purpose is
quite different. In Isaiah 55:8, "For my thoughts are not your
thoughts, neither are your ways my ways, saith the LORD." The
prophet could not have been more correct! God often divinely or-
chestrates our perceived purpose into his ordained purpose.

The Need for Purification

Purification is vital to our purpose and Christian lives. Without continual purification, destiny can be denied. And we could miss our appointment with the King! No one knows purification like Queen Esther. Purification is like the old-fashioned washboard process. The washboard process is symbolic of what is allowed to happen to us in trials, tribulations, suffering, pain, and joy. God allows these experiences because our natural and spiritual character needs to be developed. Nothing prepares us for purpose like trials, tribulations, and trouble. Forget the degrees, classes, seminars, and the conferences they falter in comparison.

A Historical Purification Process

The washboard was invented during the nineteenth century to wash clothes. The washing instrument removed all forms of dirt and impurities from clothes. The original washboards were created with wooden ridges. Clothes were rubbed upon or against the corrugations imbedded within the wood. To effectively clean the clothes, certain materials were needed: dirty clothes, 2 huge metal pans, cleaning solution, stove or heating mechanism for heating and boiling water, clothes basket/container, clothesline with clothespins and/or drying rack. If any one of the materials were eliminated, the process would be prolonged, and the clothing might not be fully clean.

According to The Pioneer for Living Survival (2010), the washboard process involved between ten to twelve steps:

1. Heat the water in one of the tubs over a hot fire.

2. Set the other two tubs up on blocks or a tree stump side by side 10-15 feet away from the fire.

3. Make certain all tubs are secure.

4. Fill one tub with boiling water, adding cold water as needed.

5. Add white clothes to the wash water.

6. Put the washboard in the tub and rub the surface with a bar of soap.

7. Take a piece of laundry out of the water; lay it the length of and on top of the wash board. Rub soap on material.

8. With the edge of the material held in your hand between thumb and fingers, rub up and down the board with the heel of your hand, gathering and pulling the material toward you.

9. Push the material down in the water and start from the beginning.

10. Scrub each garment vigorously four to eight times.

11. Dip the garment into the water, rinse, wring out water and put in next tub filled with warm rinse water.

12. Rinse in second water, wring dry, and hang on clothesline.

Boiling and Rubbing

I love the part about the hot water being brought to a boil. Trials and tribulations do this for us. I am not sure what you think of the rubbing, I think rubbing is two-fold. Rubbing is both an appropriate touch and a touch that drives me close to insanity! The appropriate touch is one that comes from a loved one that is comforting and loving. Oh, but that rubbing touch that aggravates are the uncontrollable situations and circumstances that invade your life. These situations often turn your life up-side down and right-side up, simultaneously. All of life's obstacles have specific purposes permitted by a loving, all- knowing God.

The Two-Directional Cycle

The scrubbing and pulling during the washboard process are symbolic of how we feel in process. It can seem like we are being pulled in two different directions. Have you ever thought, I cannot go backwards, but I am too afraid to go forward? This was the story of my life. I knew if I went backwards, I would be disobeying God. But, going forward was horrifying. So, I learned to look up! When undergoing your process, take a lesson from the prophet Micah 7:7, "Therefore I will look unto the LORD; I will wait for the God of my salvation: my God will hear me." Looking unto God, will keep us from insanity and forfeiting the purifying process that is needed for our purpose.

The Cleansing Agent

The most important steps in the washboard process, are the cleansing products and the procedures that remove impurities. Alleviating, the cleansing solution could result in wrinkled, wet, still dirty clothes. It is hilarious that the cleansing solution is liken unto the Word of God. The Word of God tells us to be cleansed by allowing the Word of God to wash us inside out so we can be glorious (Ephesians 5:26, author's emphasis). Think of it this way, the process helps sanctify us. We are sanctified through the truth of God. His word is truth (John 17:17).

During the washboard process, the soap is rubbed against the board and then rubbed on to the garment. We must be engulfed in the Word of God in order to respect and endure the process. The rubbing of the soap against the corrugations ensures that the backside of the garment is cleansed while the front side of the garment is being worked over by the hand. Can you picture the hand of the Lord, washing you thoroughly through His word? When our trials and tribulations (scrubbing mechanism by hand) are working us over, we can find refuge and grace to help us in times of need, distress, financial meltdown or worse. I have learned to go straight to my knees and to the Word of God when the process of purification is working the dirt out! For every situation God's word has a solution.

The Rinsing and Drying Cycle

The final steps in the washboard process are the clothes being rinsed and hung on the line. When we learn to respect the process and allow the Word of God to do its work in our hearts, we become rinsed. When clothes are hung on the line, everyone can see them. When God finishes processing us, He often puts us on display. Are you willing to endure the process required for promotion? God delights in putting us on display.

The Purification of a Queen

Queen Esther endured both physical and spiritual purification before her destiny was fulfilled. Her destiny was two-fold, she appeared before the king and was used as an agent of the King of Kings. Can you unknowingly endure a process that leads to deliverance of a nation? I know you are shaking your head, yeah whatever! I have learned and love that God *does not change.* If He used Esther to save her people, will you allow him to purify you to save your people? The story of Esther is powerful. God used Esther to turn tragedy into triumph. Esther lived with her cousin, Mordecai because both her parents died. The Bible does not record what happened to Esther's parents, only that Mordecai raised her as his daughter.

THE POWER OF PROCESS

The story of Queen Esther opens up with King Xerxes who
ruled Persia. The story is set during the beginning of the first
Jewish exile from captivity to Jerusalem. King Xerxes is holding a
feast to display his riches, glorious kingdom, and his excellent
majesty. While the king is having his party, Queen Vashti is having a party as well. Sometimes girls just want to have fun, and
how dare her husband crash her party! As the king displays his
entire kingdom, he requests for Vashti to come before his presence. It was customary that when the king called, everyone appeared front and center. If they refused, they were killed. King
Xerxes calls for his wife Queen Vashti, to show off her beauty.

Most women would be flattered, but not Vashti. **Side note:**
Some historians believe Queen Vashti's name is a modern Persian
name which means "beauty", or goodness. Everything about her
was beautiful, except her attitude. God is not concerned about our
outward appearance. He sends a special message to women in
Proverbs 31:30, "Favour is deceitful, and beauty is vain: but a
woman that feareth the LORD, she shall be praised.

I am thankful beauty is irrelevant to purpose. God looks at the
heart. Queen Vashti's refusal to oblige enraged the king. The
King sought counsel on how to discipline her. The wise men ad-
vised King Xerxes to discipline her properly, because her behavior
could wreak havoc and cause all other women to displease and
despise their husbands. Vashti must have been related to Eve, one
decision caused all women to experience pain in childbirth, submission, and obedience unto their husbands. Wow! I wish someone were there to whisper in Vashti's ear, "Please think about
what you are doing." King Xerxes took the advice of his counsel-
lors and made a decree to remove Queen Vashti. Disobedience has
expensive consequences, sometimes fatal. Not only was Queen

Vashti removed from her position, but her royal estate was also promised to her replacement. Her disciplinary actions were public and translated in every language. Ironically, her consequences did have a positive impact, it ensured that every woman respected her husband. After King Xerxes recovers from his anger, his servants recommend he look for a beautiful virgin. King Xerxes appointed officers to send a clarion call for potential queens. Each potential queen, reported to the house of women and the custody of Hedge, the king's chamberlain, and the keeper of the women. A chamberlain is charged with the management of the living quarters of a sovereign or member of the nobility. The purification process began at the house of women. It was intense and required before any woman could appear before the king. Why would anyone jeopardize their position after they survived the process? Queen Vashti had a case of selective amnesia, I am sure after she was banned from the kingdom, she kicked herself! I am not sure about you, after going through the grueling processes for kingdom work, I will not allow myself or anyone to cause me to forfeit my destiny.

The Healing Power in Purification

Before appearing before the king, the women had to undergo a mandatory year-long purification process. The purification process included six months with oil of myrrh, six months with sweet odors and other things that were necessary for the purification. Myrrh oil comes from a small tree that can grow up to 5 meters (16 feet) high with light bark and knotted branches, few leaves, and small white flowers. It is native to Somalia, Arabia, and Yemen. Myrrh oil has a warm, slightly musty smell and is pale yellow to amber in color. This oil has some very distinct therapeutic properties such as anti-catarrhal (*catarrh is the inflammation of mu-*

cous membranes, especially in the respiratory tract, accompanied by extreme secretion affecting the nose and throat) anti-inflammatory, antimicrobial, antiseptic, astringent, balsamic, expectorant, fungicidal, sedative, digestive and pulmonary stimulant, stomachic, tonic, uterine and vulnerary.

It is interesting that myrrh oil works for conditions consistent with the female body. It treats boils, skin ulcers, bedsores, chapped and cracked skin, ringworm, weeping wounds, eczema, and athlete's foot. It promotes menstruation (to ensure their virginity), relief from painful periods and it eases difficult labor in childbirth. Wow! I wish I had myrrh oil before I gave birth! Myrrh oil was poured into bath water and aided in the release of bronchitis, catarrh, colds, coughs, and infections.

Getting the Stench Out

The purpose of the sweet odors in the house of women was to purify any odors that may be secreted through sweat. Because the king's decree included young virgins from the entire kingdom, it included women from all socioeconomic backgrounds. Poor women did not have access to the purification agents that were provided by the house of women, nor did they have access to their diets. Therefore, bathing in the sweet odors helped purify their bodies of the odors that could be secreted through the skin. The historical reason that this process endured for twelve months was to ensure that the women selected were virgins. How scary to go through the process and realize you endured in vain because you did not meet the qualification!

The Cleansing Power of Purification

As God did with Esther, God requires cleansing and purification of us. Before God uses us, we must go through purification. Our purification consists of bathing in trials, tribulations, trouble, and suffering. Suffering produces the oil of God's anointing. Like the myrrh plant process to secrete the oil, our trials and trouble help us secrete oil (anointing in disguise). God must process us. The oil of myrrh makes the skin flawless. Trials and tribulations make our faith flawless. The bathing in the sweet odors gets the stench out, suffering helps weed out the superficiality in our character and faith which is useless to God.

Purification, suffering, and affliction teaches us the ways of God. When we pass the test of purification, God can use us for the big assignment He planned. When we can go through purification without whining, complaining while maintaining integrity God can trust us to deliver His people! After Esther completed her purification process, she found favor with the king. God grants us favor and "access" after we have endured the chastening of the Lord. God would not process you unless you were created for greatness. God will get out of you what He put in you. He desires His glory to be manifested in your life. If you are going through some rough valleys and roads there is good news. God is preparing you for *such a time as this!* Endure the process of purification; it is necessary. The purification process is preparing you for your destiny and it will be worth every pain!

CHAPTER 5

SET APART

"Therefore, Come out from them and be separate, says the Lord.
Touch no unclean thing, and I will receive you. And I will be a
Father to you, and you will be my sons and daughters, says the
Lord Almighty."
2 Corinthians 6:17-18

Separation can be both painful and joyous. This is the most bittersweet of all processes. Separation is the act or state of moving or moving apart. Separate in Greek is aphorizō, which means to mark off from others by boundaries, to limit, or to separate. In Greek, separation is both positive and negative. Negatively, the word means to exclude as disreputable. Positively, it means to appoint or set apart for purpose. God decided we should experience both sides of separation. Separation reveals our motives for obedience. Wow! Sometimes, we welcome separation if we think we are going to be the next Kingdom superstar. But what is the outcome when God requires separation simply because He asked with no promise of a fabulous platform? Will you separate from the familiar to the unfamiliar just because God asked? Why does God use separation to process us? Often the environments that we are accustomed can hinder the purpose God wants to birth through us. God requires separation from the world and separation from ungodly lifestyles. You cannot please God and fulfill purpose living an ungodly lifestyle. Anything contrary to God, His ways and His Word is engaging in ungodly living. We must separate from the works of the flesh and all unrighteousness. In Galatians 5, the Bible is clear on the works of the flesh. If you are comfortable indulging in the works of the flesh, just know they will definitely impede your ability to hear God. God has always required a lifestyle of holiness and sanctification. When we choose ungodly lifestyles, we are saying God's ways are not important. What I love most about God, is that His arms are wide open when we make steps toward Him. He loves us even when we outright ignore Him. Transitioning from familiar to unfamiliarity is crazy hard. But when and if, we trust God and separate at His directing, then we can access the blessings that accompany obedience. We are sons of God, right? Then we must resemble our Father. Separating from sin is acceptable for most, but what about family and friends? I know you are thinking, she is kidding, right? But, in order to really hear God and obey fully, separation is inevitable. Cutting the apron strings from family can rip your heart out.

God called Abraham, Moses and the twelve apostles to leave their families and follow him. He required it of Jesus. We are no different. When God called Abram in the book of Genesis 12: 1-3, "Now the LORD had said unto Abram, Get thee out of thy country, and from thy kindred, and from thy father's house, unto a land that I will shew thee: And I will make of thee a great nation, and I will bless thee, and make thy name great; and thou shalt be a blessing: And I will bless them that bless thee, and curse him that curseth thee: and in thee shall all families of the earth be blessed" God instructed Abram to leave his country, his kindred, and his father's house. If we intend to please God, we must obey

His voice. Do you recall when Mary the mother of Jesus, and his brothers went to look for Jesus? In Matthew 12: 46-50, Jesus gives us a glimpse of the proper alignment for families and friends in our lives. How Jesus responded to his family could be interpreted as harsh by some, but Jesus wants us to know that we must be willing to separate from our own family and align ourselves to them that do the will of God. One of the costs of discipleship is to not love anyone more than the Savior. If we place anyone over the will and work of God, we are not worthy to be his disciple. Suppose God requires you to leave everything behind to follow Him? Would you still want to fulfill your purpose, if you knew your family and friends would not understand your separation? Would you still want to fulfill your purpose, if look foolish to those you love? Or, what if your separation caused you to be classified as an unbeliever and a devil by the household of faith? Following God in the process of separation will cost, but it is worth it. When God separates you, He is searching for the seed He placed in you. He placed something in you that the Body of Christ needs.

In Acts 13:1-3, The Spirit of God instructed the prophets and teachers to set aside Barnabus and Saul for the work of the ministry. As a result of being set aside for ministry, they had special grace and were successful at what God called them to do. In the midst of their success, dissension happened. Sometimes in our prosperity, family, and ministry success, the unthinkable can happen. The unthinkable is often provoked by God to bring us to a greater place of purpose. God often uses "unthinkable situations" to draw us into greater intimacy, or even greater ministry. The Lord desires us to know and see Him more. The unthinkable can strip us into nakedness, which causes us to long for God. Then, God leads us into separation. Paul and Barnabus had already overcome many battles together. They were doing amazing. And then it happened. Paul and Barnabus begin to quarrel over John Mark. Paul thought it was useless to have John Mark accompany them on their next missionary journey and Barnabus disagreed. The disagreement between them was so heated, that they decided it was best to go their separate ways. At times, God will use contention to produce greater purpose and radical advancement of the gospel. If Paul and Barnabus had not separated, the woman who was possessed with a devil would not have been delivered nor the Philippian jailer saved. The separation of Paul and Barnabus had others' deliverance and salvation attached. We do not like to admit that huge problems, hurt feelings, broken hearts and everything that results from separation could be God! Wrong! It is certainly God's will, to get out of us what He placed in us. It is definitely God's will for the gospel of salvation and the kingdom to spread. If God has to separate us from families, friends, and churches, He will do it. When our life has been ordered by God, He may require separation to process us. Separation is inevitable.

In Job 23:13, "But he is in one mind, and who can turn him? And what his soul desireth, even that he doeth." In other words, what God desires, God will have. I do not know of anyone, who has stopped God. God is God. The process of separation is not easy, and it is painful. Separate when God requires it. Then, relax. The results are up to Him. The process of separation changed me from the inside out. I am reminded of Job 23:14a, "For he performeth the thing that is appointed for me." God has an appointment for all of us. His appointment concerns us and Him. Only God knows why He created us. God has used separation in my life to mature my faith and show me that He is enough. Radical obedience made me an easy target for separation. Radical obedience required me to separate from a career that I loved or shall I admit idolized. This type of separation provoked questions or shall I say accusations. When I separated from career, people said, you are crazy for walking away from your job. What are you doing? If I were you, I would not throw away a viable career like this and for what? The only answer I had was God told me to. Imagine how ridiculous this sounds to people who do not understand radical obedience, or just plain obedience to God. When I turned to the Body of Christ, who should understand obedience to God, I was flabbergasted by their responses. The questions about my separation from my family were hard. But nothing compared to the next separation that shook the very foundation of my faith. The faith-shaking separation came when my husband felt the leading of the Lord to leave our home church and organization that we both had been a part of since we were children. Amazingly, God braced me for it months in advance. Previously that year, God had been drawing me closer to him, urging me to spend less time with outside people. God challenged me with questions like, what would I do if I had to be alone? What if all I had was Him, what would I do? I did not get it. God allowed separation to rock my world. The decision to separate from our church family that I had been part of since I was eleven years old was pretty scary. Nothing but God and His grace prepared me for what I experienced. Dr. Dorothy Patterson writes in her book, The Handbook for Ministers Wives, "To have your character and integrity questioned is the greatest blow, especially from fellow believers." I had no clue that my husband and I, our church, and our Christian walk would be torn apart like lions rip apart a zebra for a meal. Sounds pretty graphic, huh? That is the mildest way to describe those painful months of my life as a believer.

Never in a million years, did I imagine that the people I served and worshipped with, for all those years would attack us for being obedient to God. **Unbelievable.** The most devastating part of the whole process was the people I thought who would stand with us and up for us - did nothing. Absolutely nothing. It was not because they could not, they were afraid. They were afraid that they would be subjugated to the same brutality. We endured our names being scandalized on the radio and the internet. It was so bad that people were afraid to speak to us. Worse still, even today, we have not heard from many of these people, who were part of our lives for more than twenty years. People literally left us out to dry! I feared being rejected on this level, more than anything. But God used this pain to produce His purpose in my life. God strengthened us and the peace of God ruled our hearts and minds. I was deeply saddened, because my church family whom I loved, lacked the ability to rightly divide God's word. Still worse, their cowardice impeded their responsibility to stand for truth. I learned through the process of separation, that if I suffered with God, I would reign with Him. The pastoral leaders that committed this grave offense never apologized. We forgave them. The ultimate test for me was, could I obey the word of God above personal feelings, pain, rejection, and slander. Could I pray for a person that cursed me and tried to destroy me? I could and I did. But I aged twenty years as a result of this separation. Something incredibly amazing happened to me during the separation, I had a paradigm shift. A paradigm shift is a change from one way of thinking to another. It is a revolution, a transformation, a sort of metamorphosis. I realized that in order to move forward, I would have to let go and separate myself from the painful experiences and memories. I would have to let go of the people I loved and the

THE POWER OF PROCESS

memories I cherished. To identify fully with Christ, I had to suffer this affliction. God did not remove the affliction. He changed me in the affliction and then delivered me.

In Matthew 5: 44-45, "But I say unto you, Love your enemies, bless them that curse you, do good to them that hate you, and pray for them that despitefully use you, and persecute you; that ye may be the children of your Father which is in heaven, for he maketh the sun to rise on the evil and on the good, and send the rain on the just as well as the unjust." This is God's design and His desire. It is very easy to dismiss the mistreatment of people who do not matter to you. Sounds harsh, yet true! If you do not really care, love, or have concern for someone it bothers you less or not at all. It is a horse of a different color when ridicule, lies and slander come from people you love and admire. I was blessed when I realized God ordered this separation to propel me into my destiny. Even today, I experience joy knowing that God's word considers me blessed when I am persecuted for righteousness sake. In Matthew 5:10-11, the Bible declares," Blessed are they which are persecuted for righteousness sake: for theirs is the kingdom of heaven. Blessed are ye, when men shall revile you, and persecute you, and shall say all manner of evil against you falsely, for my sake." I understand the meaning of this scripture now, but at the onset of the separation, I did not rejoice. I only felt hurt, agony and disbelief that believers could do this. I could not believe that this kind of pain resulted from us obeying the Lord.

Surely, believers would understand when God is directing you. How dare they do this to me? I thought. But God quickly reminded me that I was in no place to judge. He is in control even when things are ugly and painful. I am so thankful and grateful, that God used separation to fulfill His will in my life. This separation weeded out superficiality in my faith. Through this process, I learned that God would keep you in perfect peace. I learned that if God allowed it then purpose is attached. When God has purpose for you, He allows light afflictions. Yes, I said light afflictions. Paul told us in 2 Corinthians 4:17-18, "For our light affliction, which is but for a moment, worketh for us a far more exceeding and eternal weight of glory; while we look not at the things which are seen, but at the things which are not seen; for the things which are seen are temporal; but the things which are not seen are eternal". God considers trials, tribulations, setbacks, persecutions as "light afflictions". It has been proven that "light afflictions" do not compare to what God has planned for us when we trust Him. Embrace separation, destiny is connected. If God is leading you through the process of separation, follow Him. God is leading you to greater intimacy with Him. Do not allow the results of separation to make you bitter, let it make you better. Resist the urge to be a victim or a chronic whiner. Allow God to bless you to be a blessing to His kingdom and His people. After the separation, comes blessings. The process of separation removes everything and everyone that contaminates your ability to hear God. God is the author and finisher of your faith. The only way to know the contents of your makeup is for God to rip apart those contents so you can see you. Desire to know purpose. Desire God to use you for something special. Welcome the separation!

CHAPTER 6

OBEDIENCE IS MANDATORY

"If you fully obey the LORD your God and carefully follow all his commands I give you today, the LORD your God will set you high above all the nations on earth. All these blessings will come on you and accompany you if you obey the LORD your God."
Deuteronomy 28:1-2

Obedience, Obedience, Obedience. Why does God want it so much? I often equate this word with the giving up of myself for someone or something. I often heard this word growing up, but for me it was equated with the lack thereof. I have always struggled with obedience, I was such a strong-willed child, who grew into a strong-willed adult. As a child, I obeyed because I feared the consequences that followed disobedience. Spankings and punishments were a staple in my household, I hated *"Whoopings!"* The thought of it now brings back memories. It was not until I was older that I learned obedience had some great benefits. The word "obey" means to *carry out instructions, orders, or to comply with demands.* The word "obey" also means to behave or act in accordance with one's feelings. God wants to "persuade us" to do what He commands. He is not going to force us; He is a gentleman. When we obey God, amazing things happen. Miracles happen. Complete obedience is not for the faint of heart, obedience reveals the intentions and reins of the heart. The real challenge with obedience as an adult, was obedience to my husband. I thought we were equal. Wrong! God tried the reins of my heart with obedience and submission to my husband. With some blood, sweat, kicking, and screaming, I am better. Twenty years later, I understand the blessing in obeying my husband. I am a big girl now. I have grown so much in this area that my husband and I are surprised with how I handle things now. Obeying God can be both scary and exhilarating. Not to worry, God left a roadmap for us to follow. He did this to remove excuses like, I cannot do that! (Philippians 4:13), I am scared! (2 Timothy 1:7), That has never been done before! (Philippians 1:6), and my favorite, How in the world am I going to do that? (Proverbs 3:5-6). These thoughts may flood your mind as you journey towards obedience.

There are three distinct biblical characters that are the epitome of obedience, in my opinion: Abraham, Peter and Jesus. Yes Jesus, performed the ultimate act of obedience, his death gave life. Obedience can be scary because you do not know the outcome until you obey. God is infinite and we are finite. It is hard for us to grasp the concept of action then rationale. In our society, we must have a rationale first. This reasoning almost never applies to God unless He humors us. God loves us through our human frailty. God instructs us to do something, later, we find out why. It is none of our business how God is going to work things out, we just have to obey. One act of obedience can produce multiple miracles. Sometimes, God places a thought in our minds to do something, which we think is a good idea. Your willingness to follow through on this good idea (obedience to God in disguise) allows God to perform a miracle that you never dreamed possible.

Let us talk radical obedience, as coined by Lysa Terkurst. A radically obedient person obeys whatever God commands, irrespective of the cost. I am learning to be a radically obedient person. Abraham is regarded as the father of faith; he was radically obedient. The life of Abram unfolds in Genesis 12. God calls Abram to radical obedience. This kind of obedience was foreign to Abram because Abram was pagan and lived according to the customs of his land. Abram and his family did not serve God, so his obedience to God was unbelievable.

In the call of Abram, God gives Abram instructions. God also tells Abram what He would do because of his obedience. God does not, however, reveal when the promise would be fulfilled, or the cost of the promise being fulfilled. In Genesis 12:1-4, God calls Abram and makes His first set of promises. God promises to make him a great nation and make his name great. God promised to make him a blessing; God promised to bless those that blessed him and curse those that cursed him. God promised Abram that all the families of the earth would be blessed. Ultimately, Jesus would come through his lineage, Wow! What an amazing promise. Of course, Abram was oblivious to his connection to the Messiah. We have no clue what God will do because we obeyed. The Bible says that Abram departed. He did not ask any questions, he did not seek a confirmation, nor did he stall. This is an example of radical obedience. God said, "Go" and Abram went. My question is, "Why is it that when we know the voice of God, we struggle with doing what God said?" For the sake of argument, I propose this answer, we do not really trust God! Sounds awful. **We say we trust God with our lips, but our hearts never lie**. Abram was seventy-five years old and his wife was probably sixty-five years old, this elderly couple was settled in their life in Haran.

They were too old to travel, too old to conceive, they were just old. Abram does not look at his present circumstances, he just obeys. Side note: God did not tell him where he was supposed to go. God told him to go to a land that He would show him.

Here, is this seventy-five-year-old man taking his wife and nephew on an unknown journey. Can you imagine your spouse trying to convince you to leave everything and go north because God said go? Wow, Sarai's obedience, trust, and faith in her husband is convicting. As a young woman, I rolled my eyes at Sarai! I am embarrassed to admit, how I have behaved when my husband said let us obey God. Honestly, God did not have to tell him. If it seemed irrational to me, it was like trying to take a steak out of the mouth of a lioness trying to feed her cubs.

I am a big girl now, when God speaks to my husband about things I pray, humble myself and submit myself to his leadership. After all, the husband is the head of the wife. I have matured in my faith and my marriage; I respect Sarai's obedience. We see in the story of Abram that he sojourns through various lands and when he arrives to Canaan, God reveals more. In Genesis 12:5-7, at this point in the journey, Abram's ability to father children has met an expiration date and Sarai's womb is dead! Yet, God speaks of an impossible future. The future that God planned for us is impossible without Him. God never spoke to Abram about his current circumstance, he only spoke to Abram about his future. Only God knows your future and destiny. God told Abram that He was going to give the land to his seed; I love how Abram does not get frustrated and ask, "What about me?" Often when we do something for God and someone else reaps the benefits, we can develop a spirit of entitlement. This is why Abram is such a great example. It is impossible for you to bless others and God does not reciprocate the blessings. Abram never questions God about why his seed gets the land; in fact, he builds an altar to worship God.

In the Old Testament, altars were built to worship God. As Abram continued to travel, he went from promise to famine. Famine is an extreme scarcity of food, extreme hunger, and starvation. Historically, Canaan was the land that flowed with milk and honey. Please see this process for what it is! First, God tells Abram how he would bless him, allows him to see the blessing and then leads him pass the blessing into famine. Not only was there a famine, but a grievous famine. **Exhale**. Remember that the Word of God tells us that there are two immutable things about God's character (Hebrews 6:18). God cannot change and neither can He lie. Attention! God cannot lie! Although Abram had to go to Egypt during a famine, God's word stood. So, my friend, what God promises, God faithfully brings to pass!

Abram's human frailty is often revealed, and we see God's mercy. We are human and are guided by human emotions and we often make decisions that get us in trouble. Because God loves us, He extends mercy and an escape route back to His agenda. When Abram and Sarah arrive in Egypt, Abram out of fear asks Sarai to lie and pretend to be his sister. Because of Sarai's beauty, he was afraid that she would be taken from him never to be seen again. Abram's fear produced results; we must be careful to kill our fears with the word of God. Abram became weak in faith, but God's sovereignty prevailed. Despite this grievous famine, Abram was blessed through the hands of the Pharaoh. Even in our personal famine, when we choose to obey God at all cost, God will miraculously provide. God defies everything that stands in opposition of His plan. Pharaoh blessed Abram because of Sarai. Despite Abram's fear and lying, God kept his word. Sarai lied. God's word prevailed. Abram's heart was not to sin, but fear gripped his heart. Lying is always wrong, irrespective of our reasoning for doing it. Many times, God asked me to do things, I started out good, with pure intentions, but my human conditions hindered me. I made grave mistakes. Yet, God abided faithful! God cannot lie, he intervened for Abram, even in moral failure. God's love and mercy toward us is incomprehensible. When God promises, and your heart is right, He causes even your mistakes to work out for you. Romans 8:28, "And we know that all things work together for good to them that love God, to them who are the called according to his purpose." Hallelujah! We can mess up royally and God causes our messes to work in our favor. I am thankful. Often when God promises blessings, we often think of material blessings over spiritual blessings. In the life of Abram, God was his reward. Have you ever thought about God being your reward? If God is my reward, then all other blessings are an added bonus!

Look closely at Genesis 15:1-6, Abram questions God, "Lord God, what wilt thou give me, seeing I go childless, and the steward of my house is this Eliezer of Damascus?" Abram asks God why he is still childless when God promised him seed. Abram's servants are having children. It can be hard to watch the people around you be blessed with the thing you desire the most. Especially, when they do not really want it or disregard it as blessing. Our flesh will often try to reason with God because we grow weary. Abram suggested to God (maybe my plan might be a little better, because your plan takes too long) that he might take on the children that was born to his servants as an heir. I love how God reminds Abram of his original promise. God said, "This shall not be thine heir; but he that shall come from thine own bowels shall be thine heir." Then God stretches Abram, he asks him to see spiritually, which is very hard when you are naturally depleted and suffering. God did not just promise him biological heirs, but he promised him even you and I. God wanted Abram to understand that what He promised was greater than what he could see and measure with his senses. God's promises are so much greater. We lack the ability to comprehend the greatness of God's promises for us. Sometimes, in waiting for God to fulfill promises, we get weary. We decide that we have waited long enough, and we will get our promise even if we have to force it. Abram and Sarai did just that. They took matters into their own hands and the consequences were devastating. In Genesis 16:2, Sarai convinces her husband with such alluring words, "Since the Lord has prevented me from giving you a son, take my handmaiden and we can have children by her." Wives have to be careful not to manipulate their husbands into disobedience because they are weary and unbelieving. Unfortunately, Abram hearkened unto her voice! This couple did not foresee that trying to help God, makes a mess of other people's lives. Our obedience always has other people's lives attached. When Abram hearkened to the voice of Sarai, he involved an innocent bystander and caused her trepidation, trouble, and exile. After Hagar conceives, Sarai becomes accusatory, jealous, and judgmental. She passed judgment on Hagar when Hagar only obeyed their instructions. Abram, refused to take responsibility for his "weakness to weariness", gives Sarai the gavel to exile Hagar.

Even if people, present circumstances, or your own understanding tells you to disobey God's instructions, you will experience major heartache! When husbands refuse their leadership and responsibility, wives will be misaligned in their responsibility and wreak havoc in the family. Ouch! Husbands and wives must walk in their God appointed roles! God controls the timing of promises being fulfilled; we control our obedience. We cannot rush, alter, or end it. Sometimes, we think the promises of God are immediate. Maturity in the Lord has taught me that God's promises are yea and amen and are fulfilled in His time.

Before God fulfills a major promise or change the course of history, transformation must take place. In the case of Abram, it was a name change. In Genesis 17: 4-5, God declares the name change. "As for me, behold, my covenant is with thee, and thou shalt be a father of many nations. Neither shall thy name any more be called Abram, but thy name shall be Abraham, for a father of many nations have I made thee." God transforms Abram into Abraham and reveals the fulfillment of the promise. Abraham like us, after waiting so long, doubtfully, came to grips that the promise may never happen. This is why Sarah laughed and we laugh when God speaks of our promise again. Surely, it is impossible now, God. In Genesis 17: 17-18, Abraham questions God saying, "Really, God after we are too old to have children? Okay, I understand that you told me that, but it is too late now, just let Ishmael be the promise, he is my son." God is not moved; promises do not change because we lack the capacity to believe them. We get frustrated with God when promises and purposes seems delayed. Chill out and wait! God made the promise to Abraham, God performed the promise after He could trust Abraham's obedience. **Let me repeat that, *after God could trust Abraham's obedience*. If God has not revealed your "set time", then it could be that God is still testing your obedience!**

How many times has God asked you to do something and you did it immediately? How many times has God asked you to do something and you did it later? Guess what, doing it later is disobedience. Disobedience delays promises, I know that! When God can trust your obedience to everything He commands, then and only then will you receive the blessing. I have often heard if you obey God you will reap the benefits. They left out the fact that you must be willing (Isaiah 1:19) and you must obey God every time He asks you to do something (Deuteronomy 28:1-2). God recognizes our human frailty. He hears our heart and despite us, He fulfills His purpose in our lives. God tries the reins of our heart (Jeremiah 17:10) and rewards us accordingly. Only God can try and discern hearts. If man had to be responsible for blessing me, I would never be blessed. This is why promotion comes from the Lord. God rewards a willing obedient heart, not man, churches, leaders, or denominations. God! What happens at the appointed time? God delivers as He promised. He is not late, early, slow, or fast. He is God. I know we think that God has taken too long to do what He said, but that is impossible. He cannot lie! Numbers 23:19 declares, "God is not a man that He should lie; neither the son of man, that he should repent; hath he said, and shall he not do it? Or hath he spoken, and shall he not make it good". It does not matter what has happened, not happened, mistakes made, setbacks, lack of belief (repented of I hope), deadlines missed while waiting, persecution suffered because you believed. At the appointed time, the King will declare His glory! If your promise and purpose has not been realized yet, ask yourself these questions: Have I obeyed all that God has commanded? Can God trust my obedience? Did God tell me the set time of the promise? If you can answer yes to all these questions, where is your promise? Ask the questions again.

Peter's First Test of Obedience

Simon Peter is a classic case of how obedience and timing, regardless of the present humanity, can absolutely catapult a nation into salvation. Looking at the life of Peter, we see countless times where Peter's obedience caused miracles to take place. In spite of Peter's human condition, the power of obedience is clear. In Luke 5:1-7, we see Peter's frailty and obedience work in concert with his faith. I love Luke's account of Peter because we get to see Peter. Here, a group of fishermen who have been fishing all night caught nothing. They were disheartened and frustrated because their efforts for provision failed. Fishing was their livelihood. Without any fish, there was no money. Jesus gives Peter an opportunity to witness him as Jehovah Jireh. Peter not only witnesses the character of Jesus, but he recognizes his own sinfulness and his need for Jesus. Remember, your purpose can be delayed if God cannot trust your obedience. Jesus tested Peter's obedience by stretching him beyond his comfort zone, Jesus asked him to repeat a procedure proven fruitless. Luke 5:4, "Now when he had left speaking," he said unto Simon, "Launch out into the deep, and let down your nets for a draught." Peter's responds like most, if not all of us. Luke 5:5, "And Simon answering said unto him, Master, we have toiled all the night, and have taken nothing: nevertheless, at thy word I will let down the net." Here, Peter is saying, Master (recognizing who Jesus is), I have already done that, and nothing happened. But because you said it, I will. This kind of obedience reverences God. He loves it! "Let thy will be done!" is what you say to God, when you have reached the end of your understanding, resources, strength, power, and you obey. This is radical obedience and radical obedience ripens the ground for supernatural encounters with God. Look at what happens next. In Luke 5:6, "And when they had this done, they enclosed a great multitude of fishes: and their net brake. And they beckoned unto their partners, which were in the other ship, that they should come and help them. And they came, and filled both the ships, so that they began to sink." Imagine this, you have a need, and you obey God, and He *supersedes that need!* In a matter of moments, Peter's obedience transported him from famine to feast. Those fishermen had such an abundance of fish that their boats begin to sink. God showed himself as provider and that He was the reward! Like Peter, when God performs the miracle, we thought impossible, we end up in repentance rather than praise, because we doubted God. I will not ask how many times that has happened to you. I am embarrassed to mention how many times I responded like Peter. "When Simon Peter saw it, he fell down at Jesus' knees, saying, Depart from me; for I am a sinful man, O Lord." (Luke 5:8)

Obedience Can Reveal Purpose

God must trust our obedience before He gives us the promise. As Peter and his co-workers bring all of their work to the land, they did what most of us have never considered or learned. They leave everything behind and follow Jesus (Jehovah-Jireh). Jesus told them they would no longer catch fish, but men. Amazing! Their secular ability to catch fish was linked to their spiritual call to catch men (lead men to Christ). Peter like Abraham moved at God's command. Peter's obedience was not delayed, and the miracle was immediate. Peter was called to walk with Jesus. Jesus knew that Peter would obey even if, he disagreed. Jesus knew Peter could be trusted with things he did not know or understand.

When Jesus asked the disciples, who did they think he was, Peter responded "Thou art the Christ".

At Peter's confession of the Lord being Christ, an aspect of Peter's purpose was revealed. Look at what Jesus said unto Peter, "And Jesus answered and said unto him, Blessed art thou, Simon Barjona: for flesh and blood hath not revealed it unto thee, but my Father which is in heaven. And I say also unto thee, thou art Peter, and upon this rock I will build my church; and the gates of hell shall not prevail against it. And I will give unto thee the keys of the kingdom of heaven: and whatsoever thou shalt bind on earth shall be bound in heaven: and whatsoever thou shalt loose on earth shall be loosed in heaven. Then charged He his disciples that they should tell no man that he was Jesus the Christ." (Matthew 16:17-20.) Not only was Peter chosen to establish the church as we know it; he was given the keys to the kingdom of Heaven. What an amazing gift and responsibility, from one small act of obedience to launch out into the deep!

Obedience Opens Up the Mysteries of God

Peter's small acts of obedience prepared him for his ultimate purpose! In Mark 9:1-10, Peter's obedience, along with James and John, afforded an opportunity to see the Lord transfigured. They were trusted by Jesus. Our obedience to God shows God we can be trusted with the treasures of Heaven. Peter and his fellow disciples were given a treasure that others were not. Be encouraged, in your journey of obedience, your obedience has Kingdom benefits and at the appointed time God will reveal them to you.

Peter's Obedience Brings Salvation

Peter lived a life of obedience, even with his many character flaws. Peter had many experiences in which his obedience was tested by God. Peter responded as God knew he would. Therefore, Peter was trusted with giving birth to the Gentile nation. This pregnancy was very difficult for Peter, during this period in history, the promise of the Holy Spirit was only for the Jews. Do you think that God would ask you to do something that goes against everything you think, have been taught, and even believed? For most people, the answer would be no. God's ways are never like our ways. Isaiah 55:8-9 declares, "For my thoughts are not your thoughts, neither are your ways my ways, saith the Lord." "For as the heavens are higher than the earth, so are my ways higher than your ways, and my thoughts than your thoughts." The encounter Peter has on the rooftop, while in prayer is a clear indication that Peter's thoughts did not line up with God's thoughts. In Acts 10, a man by the name of Cornelius, whom God considered to be devout, gave alms to the poor and continually prayed. The lifestyle of Cornelius got the attention of God. God wanted to pour out his Spirit upon him and his household. God chose Peter as the vessel of honor; Peter could be trusted. Peter's obedience to God, demonstrated that he would obey irrespective of the cost. As the story unfolds in Acts 10, God appears to Cornelius in a vision and tells him that his prayers have come up as a memorial. God did not reveal to Cornelius the miracles that were about to collide with his life. God instructs Cornelius to send men to Joppa to find Peter, and Peter would tell them what needed to be done.

When God is about to work a miracle in your life, God gives very clear, distinct instructions. Obeying the instructions is the prerequisite for the miracle. God knew that Peter would be in prayer. I believe that it is the humorous side of God to interrupt our prayers and plans, to bring about his plan, albeit frustrating to us. Acts 10:9-17, describes Peter's conversation with God. Peter's humanity is very much like ours, especially when God requires us to do something uncomfortable. When God requires us to be uncomfortable, we often struggle. We may even discount it as God or better yet believe it is the DEVIL! Why? We assume God would never ask us to do something that seems contrary, crazy, or down-right foolish. Look at Peter, when God tells him to partake of what he sees in the vision, Peter responds with No. Wow! God knows Peter and Peter will obey; feelings do not hinder Peter's obedience. God rebukes Peter for his disposition, yet he trusts his obedience. Sometimes, what we think is not God is *All* God! Every person in the Bible did not obey God immediately. Some did and others like Peter did not, and God still used them greatly. God showed Peter this vision three times, Peter obeyed. Peter embarks on a journey that he does not understand, but God does. As Peter walks in obedience, he gets the message at the appointed time. When Peter meets Cornelius, the story unfolds more clearly to Peter. Often, on our journey through obedience it is not until we get to certain spiritual landmarks that God brings revelation. When Peter and Cornelius talk, God reveals His plan to Peter. Peter now understands that his assignment was two-fold. Peter realized that God is not a respecter of persons. Peter recognized that his assignment was to preach Jesus and that these persons (whom Peter called unclean) would receive the Holy Spirit. What I appreciate about God is, that He works the beginning, the end and clues us in around the middle. He knows that if He shows us His real plan, we will run as fast as we can, without looking back. I remember when God was maturing me in certain areas, I avoided obedience by simply saying, "No, thanks God! I am good." God showed me possible suffering, and that was not a part of my plan. Peter preached Jesus to Cornelius and his household, and the most amazing miracle occurred. The Bible declares that while Peter preached the Word, the Holy Ghost fell (Acts 10:44). Awesome God! A whole nation was born again because two people obeyed God. Most importantly, Peter obeyed when he did not agree or understand. Peter's obedience is why we experience the power of the Holy Spirit in our lives today! Thank you Jesus! What if your radical obedience (do not agree and really do not understand) caused changes of Biblical proportions? Not only did the Gentiles receive the Holy Spirit, but they were also taught on the importance of baptism. The kingdom of God was opened to them that day. Deep down inside of every living creature, there is a yearning to do something of significance and become someone of great value. This is the plan of God. To be and do what God desires, will cost you more than you want to pay. To whom much is given, much is required. Will you obey God even if He asks you to do something you do not agree with or understand?

Jesus, the Epitome of Obedience

The word *epitome* is defined as a representative or perfect example of a class or type. Jesus is the epitome of everything. He is perfect. Jesus was tempted in all areas as we are and did so without sin (Hebrews 4:15). All of the actions taken by Jesus represented perfection even when He rebuked sin. God is such a great God! He sent the Word to be our perfect example! *The Word* was sent to guide and show us how to obey God even if it costs us our lives!

On my journey of obedience, I have realized that God and I have very different versions of obedience. Most of us only obey because we seek a reward. In actuality, obedience is more about death and the resurrection of your life than blessing. Obedience to God means coming to the end of "you". Jesus demonstrated this kind of obedience. Hebrews 5:8 declares, *"Though He was a Son, yet he learned obedience by the things he suffered."* Chew on those words, how do they taste? Jesus, being the Son of God learned obedience by what He suffered. People love to throw around these words, "Just obey God!" But most people do not know what they are saying. Are you willing to embrace suffering? What? Are you kidding me? I challenge you to welcome suffering. Christ did, and we should follow His example. Jesus knew that His purpose was to fulfill the will of his Father, irrespective of the cost. Jesus' cost was death, God is not asking us to die physically, in most cases. Only those precious saints that God has appointed to be martyrs do that. I realize how ridiculous; I sound when whining to God about my process. Admittedly, I have shaken my fist at God for taking so long to show up! I thank God for His mercy. He loves me in spite of my sinful self! In moments of weakness, the Holy Spirit reaffirms His love and perfect plan for my life. It was prophesied that Christ would save His people from their sins. Unlike Christ, we were not sent to die for all unrighteousness, but we were sent to die for the cause of Christ in our lives and generation.

Let us observe the life of Christ and how he learned obedience through suffering. Christ was born into a family during a time and season where His very presence produced rejection. When

King Herod learned that Christ was born, he set out to kill him. If that is not the highest level of persecution! While Jesus was a baby, He became a world traveler just to stay alive. His ministry had not even begun, yet enemies of the cross wanted him dead. Jesus was consecrated to the temple of the Lord and began to do the work of His Father. After the feast of the Passover, his parents left for Jerusalem, but Jesus stayed behind. Personally, I believe this was the first rejection he received from His family while was doing the will of God. In Luke 2:48-51, "And when they saw him, they were amazed: and his mother said unto him, Son, why hast thou thus dealt with us? Behold, thy father and I have sought thee sorrowing. And he said unto them, how is it that ye sought me? wist ye not that I must be about my Father's business? And they understood not the saying which he spake unto them. And he went down with them, and came to Nazareth, and was subject unto them: but his mother kept all these sayings in her heart." Although, we do not hear Mary say anything, the scripture reveals something, Jesus became subject to her request. Something about Jesus and what He was doing bothered her. We can see from Jesus' response that He intended to obey His heavenly Father despite what His (earthly) parents thought. Much of the life of Jesus is not revealed to us in scripture, but we see Jesus' obedience with the inception of His ministry. Some Christians think obedience to God exempts them from being tempted by the devil. Wrong! When God is taking us on a journey of radical obedience, we will often end up in the wilderness to be tempted. The difference between us and Jesus is the absence of sin. We will sin, screw up, fail and everything in between demonstrating our real need for grace and the power of the Holy Spirit. Why? Enduring process without grace and the power of the Holy Spirit can lead one into pride.

We need grace and the Holy Spirit to walk out the purpose of God in our lives. As Jesus was led into the wilderness to be tempted, the devil (with his cunning self) misinterpreted scripture to Jesus (the Word). The devil knew if Jesus completed His process, salvation was inevitable and the veil that divided God from His creation would be restored. That would mean His eternal damnation. We can outlive whatever the devil offers in exchange for our obedience to God. The devil understands the power of obedience, he will use anyone and anything to distract us from obeying God. Obedience to God is more powerful than anything Satan has to offer. The devil will not stop trying to temp you; that is his job! Our job is to resist him with the Word of God. From the scriptures, Jesus' temptations show us the importance of knowing and understanding the Word of God. The devil understands God's power and he desires to cut the flow of God's power in our life through disobedience. When we overcome the temptation of position, to serve our own self-interest; to attain power and glory over suffering and the cross; to accommodate people rather than obedience to God, then and only then can we walk in the power of the Holy Spirit. The devil deceitfully tempts us with what God has already promised.

Let me give you an example, the devil, at times, tempts married people with adultery because they perceive they are lacking fulfillment in their marriage. Rather than surrender the problem to God in prayer and follow His leading, couples often fulfill the lust of their own flesh. Jesus knew His job was to offer salvation and redemption. Jesus performed every task with the spirit of excellence. Everything Jesus did either cost him rejection or rendered him praise. Funny thing, those who praised Him, were the same ones who crucified Him. Obedience to God may produce

similar results in your life. If you cannot handle rejection, persecution, ostracism, and outright evil works at the hands of men,
you might not obey God. I am not talking about cute obedience; I
am talking about obedience that makes the people closest to you
reject you and scandalize your name. I have learned obedience to
God is expensive, but so worth it. The bittersweet beauty of obedience are the amazing lessons yielded from suffering. To everything there is a time and season, but to obedience there is process.

The Process of Obedience

God walks us through process when He calls us to obedience.
Process is a series of actions or steps taken to achieve an end.
From a Biblical perspective, process in Hebrew is "rab" which
means much, many, great, abounding in and greater than. When
we go through the process of obedience, it will be great, we will
have to abound. Obedience pushes us to do the unthinkable, seemingly unbearable, and breakable limits. God starts us with small
steps of obedience, He knows our human condition and what we
can endure. Just as Jesus tested Peter with the casting of his net
into the sea, we will have similar encounters. When we are tested,
we respond with a yes or we disobey. When we disobey God, we
can still live our lives, but we miss living a life filled with God's
promises. Disobedience forfeits abundant life. Why settle for good
when you can have great? Obedience is scary, but it is the most
rewarding decision you will ever make. What is the desired end of
obedience? Is it riches and wealth? Is it a perfect life with no
problems? Is it a life of peace and tranquility? No, it is a life of
fullness of joy and perfect guidance. Only when we surrender and
obey God, will we know fullness of joy. God has in mind not to
harm us but to give us hope and a future.

Gaining Clarity

Clarity is the quality of being clear; transparent to the eye; or clearness. Clarity is not a biblical term per say, but it does have a biblical connotation. In Proverbs 4:7, the Word declares "that in all thy getting, get understanding." So many people misquote this scripture. We need to get understanding, not an understanding. Unfortunately, if you get *an* understanding, it is possible there will be misunderstanding. We need to get understanding so we can fully comprehend what is being asked. Then we are able to fully complete the task. To gain clarity when obeying God is done through prayer. When God asks there should be no guessing. Many of us know the voice of God but we ignore it because we do not want to obey. This has been me so many times. I have ignored God because my flesh was controlling me; and surrendering to God would make me look stupid. How many of us can admit that we forfeited an opportunity for God to be magnified in our lives because we were fearful and unbelieving? Many times, I felt like the least in my family. I am the middle child (no, I don't have middle child syndrome, I did before salvation though) I often felt slighted because I never seemed important enough, because the focus was always on the eldest and the youngest siblings. God is never concerned with our shortcomings as He is with our destiny. Remember the life of Gideon, he wanted to be sure of God's voice and he asked God for a sign. God honored Gideon. Gideon gained clarity with God by placing a fleece before God. Once we are certain that God is speaking, we must obey. There is no time to waste! Our obedience has someone, or something attached. Understand the truth about clarity, you can gain it through fasting and prayer! In no way, am I discounting safety in the multitude of counselors, it is needed in its proper place. Often in radical obedience, the multitude of counselors could speak in opposition to the obedience that God is calling for!

Walking in obedience to God

Okay my friends, here is where the rubber meets the road. Walking in obedience engulfs persecution, suffering, persistence to God and death of oneself. When we walk in obedience to God, we take several continual steps in the direction God is leading. And many will not understand. The key is to ensure we have truly heard from God. Walking in obedience to God, means continual responses of "Nevertheless, Thy Will Be Done". It is such a powerful statement. It means put up or shut up. As you walk in obedience, you will be tested. God takes us from obedience to obedience. This is the truest test of discipleship. Matthew 10:38 declares that "And he that taketh not his cross, and followeth after me, is not worthy of me." God exclaims that if we are not willing to suffer in obedience then we are not worthy of him. Why? Jesus, being a Son, yet learned obedience by the things he suffered (Hebrews 5:6). We are not above our Master; we must learn obedience through suffering. You may not want to hear that, but it is the truth. I have grappled with this idea of suffering and it unnerves me too! Who says, "Bring on the suffering!" Or who says, "Yes God, I am ready to suffer for your namesake!" Let me let you in on a little secret, those who say this might have a little tinge of pride! Why? Let's look at our Master, In Luke 22:24, when He was in the Garden of Gethsemane, he uttered these words, "Father, if thou be willing, remove this cup from me, nevertheless not my will, but thine, be done." Jesus (the Man) did not want to endure the cross but Jesus (the Son) was concerned only about doing the will of the Father. Jesus demonstrated an attitude of humility in suffering. Truthfully, if you suffer long enough, humility is inevitable. Walking in obedience means being willing to suffer and bearing your cross because your Father asked.

In the beginning, obedience will be both scary and exciting. God often gives you glimpses of the blessing as you walk! When the glimpses stop, silence seems so loud, persecution increases, rejection rises, and the prayers you pray seem to hit the ceiling ends the excitement. Then, walking in obedience feels crippling! Notice, I said *feels*. It is imperative that we establish our feelings LIE to us. Just because we feel God is not present, does not indicate his absence. Just because it seems our prayers are unheard does not indicate Heaven's deafness. Walking in obedience is the ultimate test of faith. Without faith, we cannot please God; nor can we obey Him. Abraham (the father of faith), Peter (The Rock) and Jesus (The Savior) all lived lives of radical obedience. Their walk of obedience was powerful, alluring and exemplifying. Abraham walked in obedience to an unknown God without question. Every request made by God Abraham surrendered. Abraham fell short when he thought God was taking too long to make good on His promise. Abraham could have been thinking, "God I think I might have an easier solution, yours is a little more complicated. I am already half dead and Sarah is right behind me!" Even with Abraham's shortcomings, he obeyed God even in the unthinkable. Abraham was willing to sacrifice what God gave him on the altar.

Peter, a skilled fisherman fishing all night, obeyed Jesus even when it went against all his knowledge, skill, and training. Jesus required Peter to defy the odds, He will require the same of us. Since Peter obeyed in the boat, he had faith to walk on water. Peter's obedience saved Cornelius, his household and us.

Jesus, the epitome of obedience, knew his responsibility was to redeem man back to God. Jesus preached the gospel to the poor, healed the broken-hearted, preached deliverance to the captives and restored sight to the blind. Jesus did what the Father sent Him to do. In the book of Isaiah Chapter 53, Jesus' cost of obedience is described explicitly. Jesus was despised and rejected of men, he was a man of sorrows, and acquainted with grief; and no one came to his rescue because he was indeed despised. Jesus was smitten by God!

Wow! Smitten means to strike with a firm blow or to be affected by something overwhelming. The suffering Jesus encountered before the cross was over the top, but the crucifixion was indescribable. I cannot fathom how a man could endure such torture for love. Jesus did all of this and never opened his mouth! What a standard! We need grace and the power of the Holy Spirit to obey and embrace the consequences of obedience quietly. What a challenge!

The Challenges of Obedience

There are awesome blessings promised as a result of obedience. But there are also challenges. Consider the book of Deuteronomy the "Blessing Handbook". This book of the Bible depicts all the blessings that are promised if we obey the voice of God. There are also some pretty scary promises if you disobey God. When obedience is presented like this, one would be a moron to disobey. Blessings are obtained after the will of God is done. The overtaking of blessing results from the fullness of obedience. This became real in my life, once I realized there were some challenges with my willingness to obey God. I immaturely believed, that when I obeyed God, that the floodgates were going to drown me in blessing immediately. God gives the glimpses and sprinkles to help us obey. When obedience is fulfilled, then the showers come. Hebrews 10:36 declares, "For ye have need of patience, that, after ye have done the will of God, ye might receive the promise."

The challenges of obedience include persecution, rejection, suffering, persistence in obedience, dying to oneself and one's dreams. These have been difficult for me to embrace. At times, I have shouted the victory and there are times when I have waved the white flag of defeat. My first real "radical obedience" test came when God instructed me to leave my career in education and postpone the completion of my doctorate degree two semesters from graduation. Yes! Some of my colleagues felt I was jeopardizing my life's work. Family members said, God was punishing me because I thought I was better than them (their analysis of sin in my life). A seasoned, godly, mentor believed because I was a pastor's wife of a young church that the loss of my income would hurt the church (Babylon thinking over Kingdom thinking). Personally, I was challenged with the fear of the unknown. Thankfully, I had a real relationship with God, I recognized His voice. I knew God was speaking and I worked to gain clarity. I had to make sure that _fear_ did not overtake me! Not only did I experience rejection from other people, but I also internally rejected this obedience as well. That sounds paradoxical. The truth is, I obeyed God and I was scared to death. Through the process of obedience, I became faithful and fearless. As God designed in His Word, the only person that stood with me in the decision to be radically obedient was my husband and rightfully so! Remember, God tests us in stages of obedience! The second test of obedience produced more rejection, God was instructing me to start a ministry for ministry wives. Who? Me? (By His Side Ministries, is multicultural and interdenominational ministry for both pastor's wives and minister's wives). During this season of this obedient walk, my husband and I were part of a **certain** denominational sect. When I shared what God was saying to me with my senior pastor's wife, I experienced rejection from her that left me speechless. She spoke as if By His Side Ministries depended on her approval rather than the anointing of the Holy Spirit and God. She told me the ministry would never be blessed. Can you imagine having to obey God and the people you trust for spiritual counsel and wisdom reject you? Hurting, I went back to God (to gain clarity). God said proceed with the launching of the ministry. Still, my trusted godly mentor, believed I was ahead of God and needed to wait. Remember, we discussed sometimes, when God calls you to a season of radical obedience, you may find "scissors" in the multitude of counselors! I proceeded despite the rejection. God knew I needed more confirmation, He provided me with the glimpses of His blessings through provision and peace, remember I was without a job! When something is God's will, it is also God's bill. To launch the ministry we needed a facility, God blessed us with a facility free of charge, the speaker paid her own way and then sowed a financial seed into the ministry, food was donated and very little out of pocket expenses was needed. Jehovah Jireh made His presence known. The miracle of obedience resulted in a sweet pastor's wife receiving physical healing. I love God. My mentor (who told me I was moving too fast and it might not be God's will) was present in the meeting. After the first meeting, she repented. I admired her humility. When we purpose in our heart to do the will of God, persecution is part of the process and it is necessary.

Persecution means to pursue with harassing or oppressive treatment because of religion, race, or beliefs. You would not think Christians would harass each other for doing the will of God would you? Mmm, wrong. It is terrible how members in the Body of Christ harass each other. It is ugly and it sends a terrible message of division to unbelievers. Remember the Pharisees and Sadducees. The spirit of pride and religious strongholds cause believers to persecute other believers. It is amazing how brothers and sisters with the same Daddy, shun each other for being obedient to their Father God. Jesus showed us how to handle persecution. It is much easier to endure persecution from unbelievers. It is more detrimental when it comes from your personal family who are believers. Wow! I never thought that could happen. When I purposed in my heart, to obey God irrespective of the cost, boy was I surprised. I am so thankful for the Word of God, it is sustaining.

In Matthew 10:22, Jesus declares, "And ye shall be hated of all men for my name sake; but he that endureth to the end shall be saved." If you endure the persecution to the end, God promises to save you. They are so many instances in scripture that support the obedient servant in the face of "mean men". When you are persecuted for obeying God, the persecution is not really (in their ignorance) directed at you but God. Hmm! Think about that, when you and I reject something that God has anointed, we have rejected God! Ouch! Put in those terms, it should bring conviction. My friend be not dismayed, persecution is part of the process it is like the meat in the sandwich. If your Christian life does not make someone uncomfortable, then I wonder about your cross. The cross itself brings persecution, rejection, suffering and death (self and dreams). But we must persist in obedience in face of the opposition.

Rejection is another challenge to obedience. Rejection means to refuse to have or accept. We can get so "fleshy ugly" that we reject people and dismiss them because they do not meet our standards. Our standards for obedience are not God's standards. After all, when did we die for salvation? We have zero to do with a fellow believer's walk with the Lord, especially, in obedience. When did God say we need another person's permission to obey His will? Help us all, Sweet Jesus! I have read the Bible from cover to cover many times, and I somehow missed that scripture. I read that we should obey God rather than man. Radical obedience to God has taught me that. Jesus, our perfect example, experienced an enormous amount of rejection from the people he grew up with, probably some relatives, and friends. When Jesus went into the synagogue to read from the book of Esaias, you could probably feel the rejection in the room. Jesus shared revelational knowledge about himself and sat down. The Bible, says that the people in the synagogue (carnal Christians) were filled with wrath, rose up, and thrusted him out of the synagogue. They led him to place on the hill where he could fall to His death. All Jesus did was declare the word and the people were ready to kill him. Thankfully, Jesus escaped. The hearts of men are wicked. They were wicked during Jesus lifetime, how much more wicked are they now. Our obedience to God can cause intense wrath in our circle, particularly when they do not understand your relationship with God; and they should not. When God calls you to obedience, outside of your customs, clichés and societal norms, things can get pretty ugly. It is unfortunate that some present-day Christians operate like Pharisees and Sadducees. Lysa TerKeurst, writes in her book, "Saying Yes to God," that she wished there were signs over people's head to let us know they would be a dream killer! Think about this, when you are approached, the neon sign would say "Opposition to the Call of God on your Life". Then you would be prepared to pray, rather than defend.

The pain of rejection and persecution produces power because it pushes the believer in a posture of consistent prayer. Consistent prayer always allows the Holy Spirit to operate more freely and fully. The pain only comes from the people who do not accept God's will for your life, you will eventually get over it. You never have to defend God's will in your life, your defenses only create strife, bitterness, and ugliness. Remember, God is for you. If your obedience offends other people, you should not apologize for it. But, if you offend someone because of your flesh, you need to apologize. The problem for most people is discerning the difference. Jesus, our Savior was rejected by His kinsmen. We must be willing to accept rejection from our family, friends, and people we admire. Radical obedience makes people uncomfortable. They are not personally rejecting you; they are rejecting God. Their rejection is most likely laced with ignorance, religious strongholds, or self-righteousness. We must stay aligned with God during times of obedience, we do not want to make matters worse by being super spiritual! Super spiritual people can be nasty, prideful, and often think people are rejecting them. Nope, **haughty spirits** make believers repel like RAID does roaches, even when they love you. We have to check ourselves through the lenses of prayer, fasting and God's Word.

Often, those who are rejecting and persecuting us have no idea what is going on behind closed doors. The word "suffer" means to experience or be subjected to something that is bad or unpleasant;

patiently or willingly. Jesus suffered willingly, but most of us complain every step of the way. Hmm. Why do we complain when we gave our life to Him? We complain because we are human, we are not in our glorified bodies and we need grace and the power of the Holy Spirit. We do not really know God until we suffer for His name. Why? Paul a prisoner of the Lord, endured an enormous amount of suffering, yet had a powerful and effective ministry. Paul wrote in Philippians 3:10, "That I may know him, and the power of his resurrection, and the fellowship of his sufferings, being made conformable to death; if by any means I might attain unto the resurrection of the dead." These words pierce my soul: power, fellowship, suffering and dead. Wow! In the Bible, the more the New Testament church was persecuted and rejected the more the gospel spread. I am inclined to believe, that the more we are pressed because we obey God, the more power God gives us to do His will. Fellowship of his suffering, what does that really mean? Fellowship means the sharing of one's experiences. When we fellowship in the suffering of Jesus, as Paul describes we share in his persecution, rejection, shame, and death (to our own will). No one wants to be talked about, lied on, and ostracized by loved ones, or give up their dreams, especially for someone else. When you become radically obedient, you are partaking in the Lord Jesus' suffering. Obedience might cost everything, but you must obey without weariness, bitterness, or offense at God. Meet the challenges of obedience without opening your mouth. Please, understand you may not see the miracle of your obedience immediately.

In Galatians 6:9 the Bible declares, "And let us not be weary in well doing; for in due season we shall reap if we faint not". While you are doing good and obeying all that God has com-

manded, you might suffer simultaneously, and it may seem that
God has forgotten you. Be persistent in your obedience. After you
have done the will of God, you will obtain the promise! We must
struggle not to succumb to thoughts of "I did what you said God,
but you allowed this. Why?" These thoughts are rooted in offense
that is directed at God, being upset with God, and frustrated by
God. Honestly, I have wrestled with these thoughts. Especially
when I *"measure"* myself and believe I have obeyed God and end
up suffering! God is so merciful, we cannot fathom His mercy. He
gives us space and time to align our will to His. Many have
walked away from God because they were offended in Him. They
waited and God did not come through, or prayers were not answered as expected. We are blessed when are not offended in
Him. Offense means to cause to sin. Do not commit the sin of offense because God did not do what you thought. God promises He
will bless you! God is faithful and if we believe Him, we will not
be ashamed. He promised in Isaiah 61:7, "For your shame ye shall
have the double, and for your confusion they shall rejoice in their
portion; therefore in their land they shall possess the double; everlasting joy shall be unto them."

God wants us to be comforted. Our flesh and the devil want us
to hurl accusations at God because we *feel* He did not keep His
end of the agreement. We have to be careful; our mouth can lead
us to sin. We can be like our twin brother Job, where we need to
ask God a few questions about why? We want to know, why?
God will answer and sometimes, He remains silent. We must
train ourselves to speak the word and trust amid the suffering.
Reward for obedience is not the goal, to be like Christ is.

The final challenge is death by obedience. I like to call it "dying on the cross of me". Dying to yourself is no picnic in the park.

It is more like placing your hands together and taking a machete and cutting your fingers off one at a time. That is excruciating pain; but when a person dies, pain accompanies it. As we are dying to our will and walking in obedience, we might smell dead flesh. You do not always know you need to kill your flesh until it shows up and it smells foul. As you walk in obedience, God will show you the works of your flesh that hinder your walk with Him. Many of us have dreams and aspirations that are not sin, but they are not God's will either. When God asks you to surrender those, dying happens. Some die quickly, others (like me) have had to die a slow painful death. I have struggled with letting go of the life I made for myself! A thriving career, working on my doctorate degree and escalating up the professional ladder. I was on top of my world. God had another plan and when He revealed his plan, I was mad. Giving up what you worked for without seeing the reward is risky. Trust has to be applied. I have to trust and walk in obedience to God daily. Some days are better than others and without the word of God, I falter. Surrendering your will can be hard, but it must be done freely. Dying to self is a life-time process. We must die and surrender daily to please the Lord. We must subject ourselves to the power of the Holy Spirit, or we will not obey. Our flesh demands our rights. The problem with our rights is they often conflict with God. To give up all and obey God is our reasonable service. He paid for us with His own blood. Wow! If we are not willing to give up all and follow Him, we cannot be His disciple.

Finally, when you are able to walk in obedience without complaint, despite the challenges, you have learned how to persist in obedience. Obedience is confirmed in the continuance. Quitting is not an option. If you continue, you obtain the promise. God honors the continuance. When you want to quit, find a secret place to pray, read and study the word. When Jesus was overwhelmed, we see Him in Gethsemane on His knees praying. Right after He finishes, an angel strengthened Him. We gain our strength by yielding to God in prayer. I cannot say that obedience to God is easy. Nothing about obedience is easy but when we seek God in prayer and rely on His grace we can obey completely, willingly, and dangerously.

The Rewards of Obedience

After every challenge there is victory. On the other side of persecution, rejection and suffering are the floodgates of blessings. When we obey all that God commands, the blessings of God will overtake us. Overtake means to come upon suddenly or unexpectedly; or to take by surprise. God promises that full obedience yields the "suddenly" kind of blessings. How wonderful! In Deuteronomy 7, God promises to love, bless, and multiply us. God promises that the fruit of our bodies will be blessed, our children and grandchildren will be blessed. Our rewards of obedience will extend through our generations. If we want to ensure a godly legacy, we must live a life of obedience unto God! God promises to bless our land. God ensures that what we produce will be blessed; nothing produced by our hands will fail! Our obedience to God is our down payment to a life of abundance, prosperity, and health. God promises healing, in fact, when we obey Him; God takes away the diseases that affected our forefathers. God promises to honor all the covenants made. God promises that we will lack nothing. God even promises that those connected to us will be blessed, no one will be barren among us. God promises us victory in the face of our enemies! Talk about rewards. Astoundingly, one act of obedience can open the floodgates of blessing in your life! Our cities are blessed when we obey God. New businesses and increased revenue are seen and felt in our cities when we are obedient. Our obedience can counteract catastrophes, disasters, crime in our neighborhoods and in our nation. There is great power in obedience.

Deuteronomy 28:6 contends, "Blessed shall be thy basket and thy store." Many years ago, my family was experiencing financial difficulty, our daughter was a toddler and we needed groceries. Previously, I heard testimonies about how God had blessed others, I knew God was not a respecter of persons. So, with my mustard seed faith, I went to the store with no money (cash) I had a check book with no money! I got a basket and went down every aisle and began to thank God for what I needed. When I got to the register, the cashier called me by my name. I do not know how she knew me, I paid for my groceries with a check! No, I did not write a bad check, I wrote the check in faith and the check NEVER cleared the bank it has been seventeen years. God even handles our enemies when we are obedient. God promises that when our enemies rise up against us, He will cause them to be smitten before our face. Our enemies will stumble before our eyes, God will fight for us. God promises to bless all that we set our hands to do. If we start a business, a ministry, or have ideas for witty inventions, God promises that it will be blessed. God promises His obedient children an open heaven.

In Deuteronomy 28:12 it is recorded, "The Lord shall open unto thee his good treasure, the heaven to give the rain unto thy land in his season, and to bless all the work of thine hand: and thou shalt lend unto many nations, and thou shalt not borrow." When we obey God, we have access to an all sufficient God. It is like having VIP access to heaven. God in His time will adjust your economic climate so that borrowing is over, and you become a lender. A borrower is a slave. When we are obedient to God, he just makes things work for us. Obedience causes time to be altered in your favor, what it takes some people ten years to do, God's favor will allow you to do it in half of the time. The rewards of obedience certainly outweigh the persecution, rejection, and suffering. The challenges are "light afflictions" in comparison to the rewards.

I know it is easy to roll-call everything recorded in the Bible. Like you, I wanted to know if God blessed real-life people. I know what I saw in the Bible; but what about my own life? Have I seen the Deuteronomy kind of blessings in my life as a result of my radical obedience? The answer is yes. I would have to write another book to roll-call all of the blessings God has bestowed upon me because of my obedience. I am still reaping from acts of obedience from years ago. One of the many blessings that I honor God for the most is the salvation of my family. There were family members that I have prayed for many, many, many years. God saved some of those family members. How amazing?! But God did not stop there! By His Side Ministries, has helped restore many clergy marriages. Ministry wives have been healed from emotional wounds that hindered their ability to effectively help their husbands walk in dominion. Wives have been healed from physical illnesses, emotional barrenness and I have even witnessed people experience the abiding presence of the Holy Spirit in their lives. Seeing lives changed is incomparable. Churches have united that were once separated by racial and denominational barriers. By His Side ministries has traveled and is traveling internationally to help minister healing to ministry couples. God is amazing.

I have experienced personal healing from wounds of the past, emotional barrenness, and an ever-increasing abiding power of the Holy Spirit. I have seen God answer prayers, while I was yet speaking, just like Daniel. Every chance I get, I share my story of obedience. Because of obedience, I have received unexpected checks, bills paid in full, divine favor and divine connections. I have yet to see all the miracles that God has in store. I affirm that obedience opens the floodgates of blessing as well as conform you into the image of Jesus. It may be scary to live a radically obedient life, but the rewards outweigh the challenges. Obey God, the rewards are both endless and priceless.

CHAPTER 7

STUDY FOR YOURSELF

"Do your best to present yourself to God as one approved,
a worker who does not need to be ashamed and who
correctly handles the word of truth."
2 Timothy 2:15

Biblical Illiteracy

Continuous travel and extensive conversations with Christians from various backgrounds, I realize we have a serious problem in the Body of Christ. We have a festering infection and Satan knows it. The more I listen to people talk about their beliefs or lack of beliefs regarding Scripture, it appears the Body of Christ is suffering from biblical illiteracy. Illiteracy is "ignorance resulting from not reading". Thus, resulting in all of the "schisms" in the Body of Christ. Not only that, but we have also disobeyed the instructions Paul gave to Timothy. We have so many anti-Christians because we the "church" have failed to rightly divide the word of truth. How can you rightly divide truth if you do not know truth? Hmm, why do we have so many illiterate Christians? Whose fault is it? The Pastors'? The Christian teachers'? Where should we place blame? A simple, but painful answer, we have Biblically illiterate Christians because Christians have chosen to be illiterate. It is never the responsibility of God's leaders to ensure that the Body of Christ rightly divide the Word. It is the responsibility of the believer.

In biblical times, the father instructed the children in the ways of God. The family had the initial responsibility for teaching their children. With the inception of American public schooling in the 1600's, children (only boys) were allowed to go to school and part of their instruction was Bible teaching. Parents willingly transferred their responsibility of biblical training to teachers. This irresponsibility sowed a seed of biblical illiteracy in the American family. "If you don't know your Bible, you need Sunday school, if you know your Bible, Sunday school needs you." This sounds great, there is only one problem, Sunday school is heavily populated with children. Children are learning but the parents are not. What are we teaching the children? We have taught them that Bible knowledge is unimportant. Where are the adults? Most children grow up with a minimal foundation of Scripture. Most children remember John 3:16. Those children become adults in the body of Christ, biblically illiterate believers. Does this illiteracy affect the spreading of the gospel of Jesus Christ? Of course, it does. A tragic result of biblical illiteracy is the separation of God's people through denominationalism, racism, gender biases and Bible heresy. It amazes me how we read the same Bible and have so many different interpretations. Who is right? I will let you ponder that in your own head!

As a Bible teacher, it grieves me to see people taught the word of God but choosing to walk in ignorance by not studying. You cannot gain biblical knowledge and understanding, by someone cutting open your head and laying the pages of the Bible there and closing it back up! Nor can you experience Bible knowledge through "eating the words" as the prophets of old. One must spend the time in the Bible, seek God for clarity of his Word and then seek to rightly divide the Word of God.

The Bible says, we should study so that we will not be ashamed! Have you ever experienced witnessing to someone and cannot recall scriptures? Have you ever been "beat up" with the Bible by a non- believer? I have and that my friend is a fatal blow! Unfortunately, too many believers have this testimony. Do you know who cheers at our biblical illiteracy? Satan. He knows more scriptures than we ever could, and will quote them incorrectly, to trip us up. That is so scary! You do not believe me? Recall, Jesus in the wilderness, the tempter (Devil) quoted scriptures to Him incorrectly. Jesus knew the Word and He was able to withstand the temptation. We lose many battles to the enemies of the cross because of our inadequate knowledge of the Word of God. Limited biblical knowledge makes us vulnerable to spiritual abuse, deception, and manipulation. Another conundrum with biblical illiteracy, is that the biblically illiterate are often ignorant of their own illiteracy. How can this be? Have you ever had a conversation with someone who declares the scriptures, says thus and so, but never found their declarations recorded in any of the sixty-six books of the Bible? For years I have heard people say, "You better be careful, the Bible says God's mercy will run out on you?" Wrong! The Bible declares that God's mercy is from everlasting to everlasting. If God's mercy is from everlasting to everlasting, then how does it run out? Have you heard "Cleanliness in next to godliness", this is also not recorded in the Bible. My all-time favorite, "Confession frees the soul", is not Bible either. This cliché comes from an old Scottish proverb that says, "Open confession is good for the soul." Biblical illiteracy is so treacherous.

Taking Someone Else's Word

If you surveyed random people, and asked them who taught them the Bible, an alarming number will say, "My pastor, Sunday school teacher or parents. Well, that is good. Ephesians 4:11-13, "He gave some, apostles; and some prophets; and some, evangelists; and some, pastors and teachers; For the perfecting of the saints, for the work of the ministry, for the edifying of the body of Christ: Till we all come in unity of the faith, and the knowledge of the Son of God, unto a perfect man, unto the measure of the stature of the fullness of Christ." God does have qualified servants to teach and minister His gospel. But why have we not come to the unity of the faith? Why does denominationalism keep us at each other's throat? Why do we take the preacher or teacher's word for it? Unfortunately, some in the Body of Christ never check to see if the preaching and teaching are in alignment with the Bible. Taking someone's word because of their position is so dangerous. The Bible admonishes us that there will be false teachers and wolves in sheep's clothing. How will we know the false teacher? How will we recognize the wolf? No rocket science needed. If the one teaching does not live according to scripture you should be concerned.

The failure to check the "message" and the "messenger" against the Word of God leads to very savage, murderous consequences. These consequences include spiritual decline, apathy, schisms in the body, manipulation, control or worse…death. The worse story I ever heard, was the story of Jim Jones in the 1970's. He was the founder and leader of the People's Temple in Jonestown, Guyana. This false teacher deceived hundreds of people with his "message". He misled more than 900 people to lethally take cyanide. This incident in Guyana ranks as the largest suicide in history. It was the single greatest loss of American civilian life in a non-natural disaster until the events of September 11, 2001. How in the world was this man able to get intelligent people like Congressman Leo Ryan to ingest cyanide? Men and women that exhibit charisma, grace and all the "good stuff" should be examined but often are not. The Bible, our blueprint, cautions us to "try every spirit" and we fail to follow through. The lack of steadfastness in God's word produces biblical illiteracy and mass suicide results. It may not happen in the magnitude of the Jim Jones days because people are more vigilant. Mass suicide happens spiritually. Why? Believers are taking someone else's word. As a Bible teacher, I love "Bereans", they show respect for the gospel and concern for their own spiritual growth. By definition "Bereans" are believers who study the Bible to gain knowledge and are able to rightly divide the Word of God. They study God's Word in context to gain an understanding of God's heart. Bereans study to understand who God is and to learn His ways. This method of studying helps to one fully understand God's will.

There will be those that have religious strongholds, residue of Biblical illiteracy or even enemies of the cross who will challenge you as you teach and minister God's word. Thankfully, God always gives us wisdom on how to effectively handle these situations. Spiritual decline happens when believers become complacent, jaded, and unchallenged by the things of God. When the teaching and preaching of the Bible becomes uninviting and unmoving, something is very wrong. Every professional must give attention to studying, improving, and practicing their craft. Believers must study Christ, to grow in Christ and do His works. Jesus shared with us His hope for His followers.

In John 14:11-13, Jesus desires for us not just to believe in Him, but to do greater works than He did. Jesus healed the sick, the lame, raised the dead and worked miracles in divers places. To do what Jesus did, we must know Him through the Word of God. Biblical illiteracy hinders powerful manifestations of God's spirit. At the inception of the Church, powerful manifestations followed God's people. The gospel spread like wildfire, miracles happened non-stop and Christ was lifted up. The more God's word is embedded in the believer, the more dangerous the believer is to the kingdom of darkness.

Manipulation and control are adjectives that describe spiritually abusive environments. I knew what manipulation and control meant by definition. But I learned what it looked like in application. I was in a spiritually abusive environment for many, many years. I was enlightened years ago by my husband. He asked me to read an article about spiritual abuse. As I read, it was as if someone had been sitting in my church, taking notes, and decided to write about it. I let out a big gasp, (**how can this be**)? I was not as astute in the word then. I dismissed it. God has a way of making sure we get the message! Several years later, a book was given to me entitled, *The Subtle Power of Spiritual Abuse*, by David Johnson and Jeff VanVonderen. This book changed me forever. I was spiritually abused and manipulated by my former pastor, and this spiritual abuse caused me to rip apart my Bible like a madwoman. I needed to understand if what I was experiencing was scripturally sound. After intense prayer, fasting and studying the Bible, I discovered that the abuse and manipulation I experienced were inconsistent with God's word. Spiritual abuse, control and manipulation made me a student of the Word.

As a result, I began to study the Bible to show myself approved(2 Timothy 2:15). I made a conscious decision to never let any Christian leader use the Word of God to bind me. Everything, I heard from that point on, I checked against the scripture. If it did not line up, I threw it out, irrespective of who it came from. Romans 3:4a reads, Let God be true but every man a liar". This is one of my life principles, I never deviate from it. It is too hazardous to take someone else's word for my salvation. The Bible requires me to work out my own soul salvation with fear and trembling. *The Subtle Power of Spiritual Abuse* was life changing and I have passed it on to others so they might experience freedom. Unfortunately, not everyone has the same thirst for deliverance and truth. The knowledge, understanding and application of the Word of God comes with responsibility. Taking responsibility might require some very difficult decisions. Responsibility can be frightening, but as believers we are responsible for what we know.

Spiritual abuse is serious. Spiritual abuse occurs when a person in a cult-religious authority or a person with a unique spiritual practice misleads and maltreats another person in the name of a deity (god), or church or in the mystery of any spiritual concept. Spiritual abuse refers to an abuser using spiritual or cult-religious rank to take advantage of the victim's spirituality (mentality and passion on spiritual matters). This leaves the abused believer in a state of unquestioning obedience to an authority. Spiritual abuse uses spiritual knowledge to deprive, torture, degrade, isolate, control or even kill others. This is why Jim Jones was so powerful. If someone tells you something about your Heavenly Father, look for yourself, to see if what they are saying is true. See for yourself, your spiritual life depends on it. Manipulation is shrewd and devious management, especially for one's own advantage. Control means to exercise restraint; dominate; or command. In essence, there is nothing wrong with control (or leadership strategies) to a degree, because some order is necessary to prevent chaos in the house of God. Control used in the context of salvation happens because of biblical illiteracy and heresy. God's true leaders never utilize manipulation and control to lead. Righteous leaders always point believers to God. If you are in a controlling situation and feel your salvation is questionable if you do or do not do something, you may be in a spiritually abusive environment. Please, consult the Word of God for direction. God requires that we fear Him, not man. God does not want us subjugated in an environment infested with manipulation and control. God is love, and perfect love casteth out all fear! Please do not take my word, their word, believe God's Word!

Know the truth. I have learned what it means to be free, really free. When God saved me, I was free from the bondage of sin. But I had to learn how to be free from past wounds, hurts, opinions, strongholds, and myself. The Word declares that "Whom the Son sets free, is free indeed." The Bible is full of truth. We cannot fully embrace God's truth, if we do not know His truth. Many do not know Bible truth because they will not study the Bible. Studying the word of God is more than just reading the scriptures. To "*study*" is to devote time and attention to acquiring knowledge; to think deeply, to inquire or research. So, we have to think deeply, reflect, and research the scriptures. Bible knowledge comes from studying. The word "*study*" in the Bible is the Greek word "*spoudazō*" which means to hasten, to exert one's self, endeavor and give diligence. The word study in 2 Timothy 2:15 means profitable. If we "study" we will profit with truth and knowledge. Having the knowledge of truth, is as important as the blood in your veins. Knowing the Bible decreases the likelihood of deception and curtails itching ears. Itching ears are a result of limited truth; when you know Bible truth everything else is irrelevant.

When you study the Word of God, you learn of God's true essence and His love. There are so many truths about God embedded in His word that absolutely blow my mind. The deep truths I learned about God and His character; I have studied. Before you freak out! I am a Bible believer, and I believe the "preacher" is necessary for hearing the word of God. But studying the word of God, is our personal responsibility and it is required. If we are destitute of truth, living in bondage, bound by strongholds, and Biblically illiterate, we are to blame. I hear people say, "I am not there yet", "I have not seen that in the Word", or "I don't know the Word like you do". In the words of my seasoned godmother, "Why not?" These statements are cop-outs and cunning devices of the devil to keep us spiritually blind. In darkness, the devil has legal access and the power to bind and blind us. When the "light" of truth comes, Satan's access is denied.

Freedom Granted by the Word

There is no reason to live in bondage, fear, or the past. There are self-help books everywhere. There are all kinds of resources available to living a life of freedom. Real freedom only comes through the word of God. In the last few years, I have been set free from the "chains" of my past through prayer, fasting and studying God's word. I do not have to live in fear of what *"man"* can do to me. Our journey with God will create enemies. These enemies can issue severe threats that incite fear. But I am fearless. People who are religiously bound think freedom means getting away from God. Actually, the contrary is true. Freedom from the ideologies of man, humanistic wisdom and traditionalism is the freedom that Christ died for on Calvary. The word *"freedom"* means the power or right to act, speak, or think as one wants without hindrance or restraint, liberty. Christ liberated us. Christ came to set us free from everything that seeks to enslave us. In John 8:36, "If the Son therefore shall make you free, ye shall be free indeed." When Jesus makes us free, no one can enslave us again unless we let them. Sounds crazy, right? It happened in the Bible, and it is happening today. In Galatians Chapter 4, Paul warns the saints at Galatia not to allow themselves to return to bondage as a result of erroneous teaching. Paul basically told them; it is "stupid" to exchange freedom for bondage. Paul used the illustration of Hagar (the bondwoman) and Sarah (the free-woman). This illustration means that the child born in bondage does not have the same access to the blessing as the child born in freedom. Consider, if you have been delivered from a million dollars of credit card debt, and you allow someone else to charge a million dollars of credit card debt again; a rational thinking person might call you an "idiot". An idiot is a stupid person or a fool. Stupid means having the knowledge but refusing to use it. Well, sometimes believers are guilty. When we share our testimony of healing, there may be people who want to silence that testimony. ***Tell your testimony so you can overcome!***

If you are silent, you are likened to the saints at Galatia. Silence is a form of darkness and as long as you remain "silent" you are bound. Life and death are in the power of the tongue, when you open your mouth to declare the works of God in your life, you are giving yourself permission to be free. When you stay out of the sin God delivered you from that is ***living free.***

The word of God can break both natural and spiritual chains. Remember, Paul and Silas in the Philippian jail. In Acts 16:25-34, these two powerful men of God were in jail bound in "chains" in the inner prison. The inner prison was the darkest part of the prison. These men prayed and sang praises unto God. Well, if you

know anything about prayer, there is power in "praying God back
His words!" Paul and Silas were singing and "praying God back
His word" and there was an earthquake. The foundation of the
prison was shaken, all the doors were opened, and their "bands"
were loosed.

God's word does not change, and He cannot lie. What happened in the Bible can happen today. If you study the Bible and
understand its power, you can be a catalyst for the breaking of
chains. When we allow the Word of God to make us free and we
testify of our freedom, other people can be free as well. We overcome our sin, trials, suffering and the devil through the words of
our testimony. And most importantly, we overcome by the blood
of the Lamb (Revelation 12:11). In Acts 16, we saw physical
"chains" being removed because of the Word. God removes "spiritual" chains as well. Recall, the boy possessed with a deaf and
dumb spirit in Mark 9:14-32. This young man who was clearly in
"spiritual" chains, he foamed at the mouth, he was cast into the
fire and water (not by himself), and there was nothing he, his father, or even the disciples could do to help. They brought him to
Jesus! Jesus asked a few questions. Jesus spoke the words, and the
young man was freed from the "chains of demonic possession".
Biblical illiteracy can barricade us from freedom.

The Power of the Word

The word *"power"* is *"dunamis"* which means strength and
power. I think of God's word "power" like a stick of dynamite!
Dynamite can blow up anything. Demons, strongholds, uncontrollable emotions, past failures, fear, past wounds, and sin are
powerless over believers embedded in the Word of God! When
ungodly things have plagued my life and the Word of God was
correctly applied, "these things" fell flat like the walls of Jericho!

The authority of God's Word applied to any situation, is annihilation by desolation. The Word is so powerful, God speaks, and it is! You will only know God if you spend time with Him. Many profess belief in Him but do not know Him, because they have not spent time with him, studied him or listened to Him.

The word of God created a world from nothing, raised the dead, cast out devils, delivered from a den of lions, caused walls to fall flat and tore the veil dividing man from His God! Now if the Word can do all of this, why live a life destitute of this kind of power? When we are trapped in the den of devastating circumstances, we can speak the Word and the circumstance will either submit to the authority of the Word, or God will transform us through the circumstance. Either way, we have victory!

When I was in seventh grade, I had a heart condition and had to wear a heart monitor. The monitor checked my heart rate. The beating of my heart caused severe pain in my chest. I knew Jesus could work miracles. I believed in His power. I remember the doctor doing all kinds of tests and I remember the pain like it was yesterday! The doctors determined that I had blood clots in my right artery which was causing the pain. The solution was open-heart surgery! Open heart surgery for a twelve-year old was pretty risky. If I had the surgery, there was a fifty percent chance that I would die. But everyone that knew me prayed. We asked God for a miracle.

The surgery had already been scheduled. I went back to the doctor and he wanted to take another x-ray. When the doctor reviewed the x-ray, he seemed puzzled. He asked the specialist to take a look. The specialist looked and they talked. They called my parents out into the hallway. I knew God had done something; I heard my mother screaming. Well, the blood clots had miraculously disappeared, and the pain dissipated. I was miraculously healed, and the doctors saw the power of God! God blew our minds that day! God has continued to miraculously intervene in my life through the power of His Word!

I believe in the power of the word of God. But there can be no power if there is no word of God! If you do not study the word of God, you will never know the power God has given you. Believers live defeated lives and succumb to a powerless existence because they do not abide in God's Word. God intends for us to live miraculous, victorious lives. God does not want His people to be ignorant of His word. In fact, in the Old Testament, the commandments of God were to be taught diligently to the children by their parents (not Sunday school). Parents were to talk about God's commandments in the house. They were to spend time in the Word and devotion (in the morning and at night). They were instructed to bind them for a sign upon their hands and a frontlet between their eyes. These instructions were to make sure that God's laws were always at the forefront of their minds, it was intertwined in their lives and passed down for generations. God required study of His word back then and He requires it now. Therefore, thou shalt not wiggle out of the studying of the Word of God. Spiritual abuse, manipulation, control, spiritual apathy, fear, bondage, and sin shall be thy reward if thou fail to study the Word of God!

Your Purpose is Connected

Have you ever heard people say what God called them to do? And wondered where in the world they got that from? If you are honest, at some point in your life, you have heard people talk about their destiny and your eyebrows raised and your lips twisted in disbelief. Honestly, I have had some eyebrow raising, lip twisting, choking moments and unbelieving laughter, like Sarah! I am almost ashamed to admit this. I was so immature and biblically illiterate and so were the people talking to me. I have matured in God now and I know God will never speak outside of His word. God will never call us to something that is not supported by His word. God cannot change nor can He lie. In Proverbs 19:21, "There are many devices in a man's heart; nevertheless, the counsel of the Lord, that shall stand." In other words, it does not matter what happens or does not happen, the counsel of the Lord stands. We seek the counsel of the Lord through His word. God's word is **proven**. The only person that knows the plans for you is the Lord (Jeremiah 29:11). We are finite beings and our mind can only handle so much. If God would reveal all of His plans for us with the process included, we would all moonwalk backwards like Michael Jackson, right out of God's will.

To trust God fully, you must have enough Word to combat the opposition that you will face. Think of the Word of God in this manner, Popeye from the late 1920's Thimble Theater, was a character who often found himself antagonized by Bluto, who sometimes bound him in chains (how ironic!). But when Popeye ate his green spinach, he was able to wipeout his opponent. Well, that is what the Word of God, will do for us if we study and make application. The devil seeks to bind us in all kinds of chains and strongholds. Arm yourself with the Word of God, so you can break chains and live free.

CHAPTER 8

❧

Hearing God Speak

"Undoubtedly there are all sorts of languages in the world, yet none of them is without meaning."
I Corinthians 14:10

An Ear to Hear

"He that hath an ear, let him hear what the Spirit saith unto the churches; to him that overcometh will I give to eat of the tree of life, which is in the midst of the paradise of God." God wants all of us to hear, understand, and apply His words to our lives (Revelation 2:7,). Why is emphasis put on hearing God? If you cannot hear God, you cannot walk in purpose. Then, how do we hear God? We talked about key processes that God uses to speak to us. Now, let us go deeper. We have heard many things about life, love, God, and everything in between growing up. The problem is that we are unsure which are our thoughts and which thoughts have been framed by others. Simply put, as a child your family has a set of beliefs that you almost always adopt. Your church has a set of beliefs with which you must comply. Society has depicted a set of ideals that you have conformed to. These structures form our thinking, our way of life and who we "think" we are. When God begins to speak "purpose" to us it can sound foreign. Puzzling, I know? The ways of God are opposite of ours.

Well, that seems pretty understandable. Right? Wrong. What happens when God begins to call you and His voice sounds really different from what you have heard, learned, and been taught? What will you do? Do you listen to this voice that you know beyond a shadow of doubt is God? Or do follow what you have always known?

Most people never fulfill destiny because of roots of disobedience, fear, and rejection. If you overcome these three roadblocks you will more likely fulfill your destiny and purpose. Most of us have voices in our heads that compete for priority. I am not advocating that the world is schizophrenic. If so, all of us would need to be on the altar asking God to deliver our minds! When we make life decisions and choices, we hear our parents, Christian leaders, closest friends, and spouses talking. With all these voices competing to help us make decisions, how can we ensure that the decisions we make are ours. We must silence every voice that is not God.

Silencing the Voices

Silence means to cause to become silent; prohibit or prevent from speaking. When you make up your mind to obey God in everything, many voices will try to influence you to disobey God's voice. Our obedience to God can cause cynicism (and other stuff I dare not mention) that will leave you speechless. You have to be strengthened through the grace of God to silence competing voices. Occasionally, you will have to do it both quietly and loudly. I have come to realize that people think they know more about your purpose than God. How can a sinful, finite voice carry more credence than God? I am still researching this answer. This sinful person can be you or someone in your circle. Yes, you! Your fear can speak so loudly that it will cancel every scripture you know and every true experience you have had with God! Your rejection can crescendo louder than a demolition blowing up buildings. Rejection will tell you if you obey, people will hate you. Everyone wants to be loved. Certainly? Disobedience will tell you; God will still love you if you disobey. It is true, but there are **costly** consequences for disobedience. James 4:17 reads, "Therefore to him that knoweth to do good, and doeth it not, to him it is sin." If you know God has instructed you to do something and you disobey, it is sin! And sin is expensive.

When God speaks to us and we are sure it is Him, we must obey at all costs. Irrespective of what anyone thinks, feels, or says. Know that God will not speak outside of His word. For example, God will never tell a woman to disobey her husband to follow Him. Man is the head of woman. If you think or "feel" God is telling you to disobey your head, please check for clarity! If you use the scripture obey God rather, than man, please check for appropriate interpretation! **Note:** Before we get into a tangent, we understand there are special circumstances. We do know we are not to obey sinful requests. In Ephesians 5:22, Wives, submit yourselves unto your own husbands, as unto the Lord." Women, in reference to special gifting, if you will honor the Word of God, continually pray, and wait on God's timing; doors for your gifting and calling will come forth. You will not have to defy your husband to obey God. If your husband is an unbeliever, honor him, God will ensure that your gifts will make room for you (Proverbs 18:16). Many women miss the beauty in this sanctifying work of God, because God's timing is always different from ours. God promises to make everything beautiful in his time (Ecclesiastes 3:11). Women, if you will wait, pray, honor your husband, God will make your purpose beautiful by sanctifying your husband through your life. The same principle is true for men. God will make room for your gifts and God's purpose for marriage will be evident in both lives.

Everything we need is found in the Word of God. The older I get, the more I embrace God's word over voices, opinions and the "pseudo-revelations" of other people. Please understand, I am not discounting wise counsel. The Bible declares that in the multitude of counselors there is safety. And through counsel we make war. But we must discern wise counsel from ungodly counsel even from godly people.

If a person speaks contrary to the Word of God, it is unwise counsel. Their position and counsel become irrelevant. God will never defy His own word! Let me explain, your individual purpose is between you and God. God will never place us in a position that brings His Word to naught! Sometimes spiritual people think it is their duty, to help you get to your destination. Getting to your "destination" is a covenant between you and the Lord. On my journey to destiny, many people believed that God "sent" them to counsel me in the direction that God wanted to take me. Some were very accurate, and some were as off as mosquito spray. Some asked me to disobey God because my obedience made them uncomfortable. I had to cultivate my hearing of God's voice to stand firm in obedience. Then, there were those whose "spiritual intuition" was in complete opposition to God's instruction. Had I not been clear on God's instructions, I would be in a cesspool of mess and engulfed in disobedience. At times, it can be very difficult to silence opposing voices. These opposing voices came from people I respected, loved, and honored. I knew that there was no counsel above the Word of God. Proverbs 21:30 proclaims, "There is no wisdom, nor understanding, nor counsel against the Lord." When God speaks, the counsel of your spouse, parents, friends, and teachers should not compete. Their voices should only confirm.

The Word is a Silencer

To silence a voice, you must know the voice of the Father. You learn the voice of God through His word and prayer. When voices of tradition, family, religious backgrounds, and schools of many thoughts compete for our attention, we must apply the truth of God's word. Silencing other voices is a spiritual battle. In Ephesians 6:10-20, instructions are given on how to silence voices that compete with the voice of God in our lives. We must arm ourselves to hear God. God's purpose for us will often oppose Satan's plans and our current circumstances. Wearing our spiritual armor helps us hear God. We must understand that it is never people that want to hinder our purpose. It is hard to comprehend this because we see and hear people. The struggle with competing voices is about the will of God being done in the Earth. Satan wants to thwart God's will. Whatever, whomever he can use, he does and often without us even recognizing him. The key to silencing him and his devices is to be equipped with the word of God.

We have all seen movies where people were silently murdered with guns, because the gun had a silencer. Every now and then, you will need a silencer. These opposing voices will speak fear, rejection, and disobedience at the most inopportune time. If you are fortified with the knowledge and truth of God's word, God's word eradicates them. Fear, rejection, and disobedience cannot stand up to the counsel of the Lord. Our battle is not a carnal one, we must fight with spiritual weapons. Paul told us in 2 Corinthians 10:5-6, that we should "cast down imaginations (fear and rejection) and every high thing that exalteth itself against the knowledge of God (anything in opposition to God and His plan) bringing into captivity every thought to the obedience of Christ. And having in a readiness to revenge all disobedience, when your obedience is fulfilled (disobedience comes into obedience through the Word of God)." Can you see how the word of God silently kills the voices that speak?

Prayer is a Silencer

What happens when speaking the word *appears* not to work? Prayer is the next move. The word of God always works, but when it appears that it does not, then we enter into prayer. Jesus was in the Garden of Gethsemane struggling with His assignment to die on the cross, he bowed in prayer. When He prayed, the Word became alive and He went to Calvary. Prayer gets God's attention. How can God speak to us? How can we hear Him if we do not talk to him? We must pray! Our prayers help us know if we are hearing correctly. God will always reaffirm you of His plan when you seek Him in prayer.

In Luke 18:1-8, Jesus speaks a parable about how we should approach God in the midst of troubling circumstances. When you are struggling with obedience to God and everything is in opposition to what God has spoken, it is extremely troubling. We should approach struggling situations with the same fervency, persistent faith, and prayer as the widow did. If we follow her example, we are guaranteed results. This widow cried out so, that her oppressor granted her petition because she got on his nerves. He did not fear God or man. This widow worried the judge into agreeing with her request. When we cry out to God like this widow, the opposing voices are automatically silenced. They cannot survive in continual, fervent, and persistent prayer to God. Opposing voices cannot handle tenacious prayer, they will submit to defeat. If you are praying and mobilizing yourself with the Word of God, the "ungodly" voices and circumstances will submit to God. Prayer works when you readily engage in it. You cannot silence a gun if you do not understand how the silencer works. That kind of ignorance can kill you or someone else. If you do not learn to silence the voices that speak in opposition to God, your purpose will die.

Silencing the Voices of Family

Jesus demonstrated in word and deed how we should hear God. The voices that give us the most trouble are our parents, religion, and our own. At times, these voices are laced with fear and doubt. Why is the voice of our parents so hard to overcome? Our parents' voice is the first voice of authority in our lives. We heard and obeyed their voice before we knew there was a God to hear. For many, parents introduced us to God. Our parents did everything for us. They aided us in growing in maturity. We are loyal to them, which can make discernment very difficult. Parents are charged by God to train children in the way they should go (Proverbs 22:6). Fathers are instructed to cultivate and nurture children in the admonition of the Lord (Ephesians 6:4). Although these are commands of God, many parents have fallen short and struggle, me included. *Interesting*.

Jesus was born to the Virgin Mary. Jesus was taught the customs of Mary and Joseph and he lived his "natural life" according to the lives of his parents. Jesus did so until it was time to fulfill his purpose. Children are charged by the word of God to obey their parents. No exception. Adults are commanded to honor their parents. Honor and obedience are two different things. Obedience means to comply with the command or to submit to the authority of another. Honor is to give high respect or esteem. To expect an adult to obey a parent is ludicrous. They are only to honor. The only adult I know required to obey another living human being, is a wife to a husband. All other adults obey God. I know that hurts, but it is biblical truth. Discerning the difference between honor and obedience helps increase discernment thereby silencing the voice of parents *when their voices oppose the voice of God.*

Jesus, the Example

Why is it important to silence the voices of parents in reference to obeying God? Many have forfeited the plan of God because their parent(s) disagreed, misunderstood, or did not support the will of God for their lives. This is tough for children because parents are regarded highly in the lives of children. Unfortunately, parent(s) can never supersede God's plan or His will. Personally, this has been the hardest and most painful thing I have had to do. When it comes to fulfilling the will of God for my life, I must forfeit the counsel, wisdom, opinions, and suggestions of my parents **when I know it opposes God**. I never thought I would have to do it because my parents are believers. Fully embracing the will of God for my life, required the severing of emotional strongholds of acceptance, fear of rejection and approval. I allowed God to break these in my life, I live in freedom. Do I honor my parents? Yes. Do I listen to them? Yes. Do I care about what they think and feel? Yes. However, when it comes to God, His work and His will, their opinions, feelings, and beliefs have little significance. It has been hard for my parents to grasp, unfortunately, there is no counsel against the Lord. ***Funny, I am being tested with my own children***. Jesus beautifully demonstrated how we should respond to our parents positioning in our lives. The writers of the gospel showed us how Mary responded when Jesus obeyed God over her. The question for us is, will we respect our children when they choose to follow the voice of God? Will we choose to be angry, dissonant or reject a relationship with them? Or worse, become offended and get in trouble with God? The answers will only be evident when we are personally faced with the situation. God has special purposes for my children, I seek Him continuously for wisdom.

Mary was chosen to give birth to Jesus. What an amazing assignment! How she must have felt knowing, her baby would become her Savior and she would have to submit to His authority! In Luke 1:8-19, Mary learns from the angels and shepherds that Jesus was coming and her role in his life. Imagine her feelings as she gave birth, nursed, and changed the diaper of her son, knowing he was called to lead her. I would love to ask Mary how she felt when Jesus honored His call over her. When Mary hears all about Jesus' purpose, the Bible states in Luke 1:19, "But Mary kept all these things, and pondered them in her heart." We can assume that Mary had feelings about what she heard but she kept them quietly to herself and pondered them.

At twelve years old, Jesus was about his father's business. By natural standards and custom, he was a child. Yet, in Jewish custom, manhood was imminent. At twelve years old, Jesus was still subject to the authority of His parents. In Luke 2:41-52, we can see that Jesus was attracted to the will of His Father. After the feast of the Passover, Jesus and his "earthly" parents went to Jerusalem. Jesus stayed behind without his parent's knowledge. They had traveled for a day before they even realized their son was missing. How is it possible to go on a trip and not realize your child is missing? Even the parents of Jesus were imperfect. Godly parents sometimes blow it real big; we need to breathe and give our parents grace. Mary and Joseph looked for Jesus for a while before they decided to travel back to Jerusalem. After three days of looking for him, they found him in the temple, sitting among the doctors talking. Everyone was amazed at Jesus' knowledge and wisdom.

The conversation between Mary and Jesus is quite interesting. Take into consideration Luke 2: 48-52, "And when they saw him, they were amazed: and his mother said unto him, Son, why hast thou thus dealt with us? Behold, thy father and I have sought thee sorrowing. And he said unto them, "How is it that ye sought me? Wist ye not that I must be about my Father's business?" And they understood not the saying which he spake unto them. And he went down with them, and came to Nazareth, and was subject unto them: but his mother kept all these sayings in her heart. And Jesus increased in wisdom and stature, and in favour with God and man." Ouch! A mother inquiring of her twelve-year-old son's whereabouts and he responds, "Do you not understand that I must be about my father's business?" In other words, he tells her that my purpose is more important than being with you! His parents were both in awe and confusion. Oftentimes, when we discuss God's will for our lives with our parents, or when we make God-led decisions they will not always agree. Understand and be okay with the fact that your life and purpose is between you and God. I cannot imagine looking for my child for days, and when I find him or her, they respond with, "Why are you upset, I must do God's will? Most of us would respond with discipline. What would you do?

When Jesus became a man, his response to his parents and family changed. In Luke 8:19-21, Jesus tells us how we should engage our family when it comes to the will of God. Families, especially parents, struggle with giving up or limiting their parental influence in the lives of their children. When children become adults, parental authority, and influence changes. Parents should only expect honor. The expectation of fulfillment of personal wishes and desires or forcing of opinions or unrealistic expectations is unacceptable and unbiblical. Luke 8:19-21 records, "Then came to him his mother and his brethren and could not come at him for the press. And it was told him by certain which said, Thy mother and thy brethren stand without, desiring to see thee. And he answered and said unto them, my mother and my brethren are these which hear the word of God and do it". Jesus laid the foundation for us. If our family does not hear and obey the Word of God, they have no relation to us. In simplistic terms, parents and siblings' feelings of disposition, opinions, comments, and concerns cannot carry more weight than what God requires.

In Luke 14:26, Jesus told the disciples that if any man come to me, and hate not his father, and mother, and wife, and children, and brethren, and sisters, yea, and his own life also, he cannot be my disciple. Sounds harsh, but God's word is the authority. God wants us to understand that family loyalty does not supersede loyalty to God. As parents, we must be careful with our words and actions concerning our children. We will give an account for them. In the Bible, God disciplined Moses' family for speaking against him. To silence the voice of parents, family, and traditions we must obey God over all. Unfortunately, this level of obedience to God may cause some rifts in relationships, pain and perhaps some separation. Know, it is never wrong to obey God fully and completely.

Silencing the Voices of Religion

Have you ever analyzed your beliefs about God? Do you have
your own opinion of God? Better yet, do you know God for yourself? For years, I pondered each of these questions in mind. I have
searched for absolute truth. I desire to know the God of the Bible
and I want relationship and fellowship with God. In my search for
absolute truth, I realized that a lot of what I believed was not
based upon my own personal knowledge but what I learned from
others. I came to the realization that not studying the Bible for
myself resulted in biblical illiteracy, which lead me into some
pretty scary situations. Desiring to know the God of the Bible, I
had to silence the voice of religion to walk out my purpose. In my
pursuit of absolute truth and according to the Bible, I had to re-
think my beliefs. My eyes have been opened to biblical truth that
was hidden from me because of religion. In some of my religious
training, I was taught that God does not use a woman to minister
his word. I was taught that you should never question the man of
God. And that you should not make decisions unless you consult
with your pastor. I was taught that women should not wear pants,
make-up, or jewelry. None of this can effectively and consistently
be supported by scripture. Yes, people can find verses outside of
the original context and make it applicable, while there are no
other witnesses in the scripture. This is eisegesis and it leads to
biblical illiteracy. Eisegesis is when an individual interprets a Biblical text in a manner to introduce their own assumptions, agen-
das and biases. People have made non-salvation issues doctrine. If
we are biblically illiterate, we become mesmerized by stunning
charisma and eloquent speech. Watch out for that! You should not

only know what the Bible says but the history and context as well.

The problem with religion is that much of it is contradictory to the Bible. Religious voices often directly opposed God's plan for my life. How could God call me to teach and operate in ministry, if it is forbidden by scripture? Why does God instruct us to obey him rather than man, if we cannot make decisions without the counsel of man? Would God say wearing pants was a sin, if pants were not even invented during the canonization of scripture? Would God say jewelry is a sin when Job wore an earring and the children of Israel had enough jewelry to build a golden calf? Did God say wearing make-up is sin when cosmetics inventors were not born? Finally, did God really say a woman could not be used in leadership, when he called Deborah to prophesy and lead the children of Israel as a judge? Crazy, huh? These questions without real biblical validity, keep purposes and people in bondage. Religious schools of thought can lead to religious strongholds. We must rightly divide the word of truth.

When God spoke the purpose for my life and I was sure I heard clearly, I had to come to grips that what God was speaking was in opposition to my religious upbringing. To obey God, I had to make a conscious decision to let God be true and every man be a liar. I decided that anyone who spoke in opposition to God's word including myself, should be considered irreputable. Harshly enough, such a decision is necessary to fulfill God's will for your life. In order to silence the voices of religion, I had to strip everything and start fresh. I had allowed the traditions of men to make the Word ineffective. I allowed my allegiance to erroneous thinking patterns to perpetuate disobedience to God. I ignorantly believed if I obeyed God, I would be in sin. How ridiculous! I knew

God was speaking but willingly disobeyed. I refused to surrender to God because of religious fear. The voice of religion carried more weight than God. This is hard to admit but it was my reality. How do you tell the religious schools of thought in your head to shut-up? You do what Peter did. Peter obeyed God although, he disagreed. Peter's obedience caused the Gentiles to be engrafted into the family of God. You silence religion by hearing and obeying God. Jesus is our example. Jesus knew His purpose. Jesus ministered to everyone including the children, who were considered voiceless. Jesus heard the Father's instruction and obeyed irrespective of the voices of the Pharisees, Sadducees, and religious magistrates. If we are going to silence the voices of religious schools of thought and walk in freedom, we must hear God and obey. Any belief that is not supported consistently and effectively by scripture must be forsaken. Forsake erroneous thinking and teaching. Follow the inerrancy of scripture, it has open enrollment, high promotion rates, non-existent failure rates and its success rate is eternally guaranteed.

Silencing the Voices of Fear and Doubt

I have consistently put a vice-grip on fear and doubt. These voices are like tornadic, tumultuous, heaven-shaking storms seeking to hinder your ability to hear God and obey. At times, fear and doubt loudly bombard us because God's timing and ours are distant cousins. When we are waiting for answers, these rascals sneak in and try to badger us to death. How do we fight back? We fight back with prayer, fasting, speaking, and applying the word consistently. If you do not have a strategy to fight fear and doubt, they will erase you and your purpose permanently. Think about it. If you fulfill your purpose, the will of God is done in the Earth.

Know, the devil is not trying to have that! So, the devil hooks up with fear and doubt and launches them against you simultaneously. They have one job, to double-team you, so you will disqualify yourself.

Doubt is the absence of faith and it is sin. Without faith, you cannot please God. Anything that is not faith is sin! Lord, help us! When you are hearing, trusting, and obeying God, doubt lies in wait like a hungry lion to pounce on you. Doubt will tell you that you are never going to see victory in your situation. Doubt will tell you that God has forgotten about you and that your labor is in vain. Doubt will even question the very existence of God. Doubt likes to kick a man when he is already down.

How do you silence doubt? First, you repent and ask God to increase your faith. Then you must speak the Word of God silently and aloud. If you need to, pray. Finally, you must praise God! You speak the word because life and death are in the power of your tongue. If you speak the Word, doubt will incinerate. Otherwise, doubt will rage like an inferno. Infernos can be painful to put out. The method you choose to speak the Word, is irrelevant, you just need to do it. The voice of doubt lowers in decibels when you pray. The word of God and prayer are strategic weapons for battling doubt. Tell doubt, "I will not be weary in well doing, for in due season I will reap if I don't faint (Galatians 6:9)." Did you know that praise damages the spirit of doubt? Do you remember the game mortal combat? I loved that game. The game used to say, "Finish Him!" There was a fatal move in this game, you could rip the bones out of the body of your opponent and he or she would fall dead! When you pray and speak the word, you leave doubt in a "wobbly" state. When you add praise on top of praying and speaking the word, doubt is finished! Praise invites the very presence of God into your atmosphere. Psalms 22:2 declares, "But thou art holy, O thou that inhabitest the praises of Israel." When we praise God, He lives in our praise. The word inhabit means to "live" or dwell". Can you imagine what happens when God inhabits anything? It is never the same! When we pray, speak God's word, and praise Him. Then, doubt is **Finished!**

Fear is crippling. Fear is, False Evidence Appearing Real. Fear tells us something is true that is always false. If we let fear talk, we can wind up in a white straight jacket with our arms tied behind our back. Fear can drive you to insanity. The Bible declares that fear has torment and is not made in perfect love. Honestly, when we are afraid of something, we are worried and cannot function correctly. Fear tries to convince us that the promises of God are falsehoods. Fear lies to us. Fear speaks ifs, and what ifs. God speaks confidently. Fear speaks rejection and confusion. How do you tell fear to shut-up? You declare, "God has not given me the spirit of fear, but of love, power, and a sound mind (Timothy 1:7)." We can powerfully combat insanity, rejection, and weakness. Fear does not have to have dominion in your life.

Praise annihilates fear just as it annihilates doubt! Fear cannot stand praise. Speak the word and praise God, you will suffocate fear. Fear competes for attention in your mind. Let, fear know that God's perfect love prevails. Fear is powerless against the counsel of the Lord. Tell fear, I praise God, no matter what! Fear knows there is nothing too hard for God, which is why it lies to us. In my spiritual arsenal, I have scriptures that specifically target fear, so when fear shows up, I launch my scriptural AK47 and blow fear back to hell. Not only that, but I am also a ridiculous praiser! I have learned to praise God when I am up, when I am down, when hell breaks loose and when blessings are overflowing. Praise is a personal invitation to God!

Hear God, Your Purpose Depends on It

We acknowledged that all these voices in our lives have significance, but none can stand against the counsel of the Lord. God's plans for you, are to prosper you and not to harm you. We must believe that God cannot lie. Circumstances and situations can make it seem like God's word is a lie. In 2 Timothy 2:13, the Word of the Lord vies that, "If we believe not, yet he abideth faithful; he cannot deny himself." God will not lie on himself; whatever God says is truth. It does not matter how we feel, what we think or what we see. When God speaks, we must hear, obey, and believe. Our purpose is our purpose. God will not share all the details of our purpose with someone else and leave us out. We will lose sight of purpose if we succumb to the opposing voices in our lives. We must have absolute loyalty to God. Nowhere in scripture does it say, we should make sure our families are comfortable with our walk with God. When God gives instructions, our comfort level must be aborted, and the relentless consulting of others must be stopped. God is the ultimate authority in our lives and His will must supersede all. It takes courage to silence opposing voices in your life. It is an expensive assignment to hear God above family traditions, religious traditions, societal norms, and personal feelings. But if you hear God in the midst of all the noise, and obey what you hear, you will be blessed immeasurably. The timing of blessing is up to God. We must ask God to strengthen us as we wait. Remember, if a voice tries to compete with the voice of God in your life, **Silence it.**

CHAPTER 9

HUMBLY TESTED

"Remember how the LORD your God led you all the way in the wilderness these forty years, to humble and test you in order to know what was in your heart, whether or not you would keep his commands."
Deuteronomy 8:2

Humility Defined

Well, we have arrived at the throat-swallowing part of our journey together. Most people wish they could bypass humility because it constitutes suffering. It did for the children of Israel, it did for Jesus, and it does for us. To understand what God means by "being humble" we must define it. You can never do something if you do not know what it is. I have truly been delivered by learning what God means by humility. People can (ignorantly) put us in bondage by their definition of humility. Our definition of humility and God's definition of humility are two entirely different things! And praise be unto God, it is! If we go by man's definition of humility, many of us including me, would never make it to the promises God has for us.

To effectively explain what God meant in Deuteronomy and every other place in scripture that you find the word "humble" and "humility" we must do a little hermeneutics! Since Deuteronomy 8 is the focal point for this chapter, we will define the word humble from both a scriptural and a natural definition. The word "humble" means not proud or arrogant, having a feeling of insignificance, inferiority, and subservience; or to be courteously respectful.

The word "humble" in the Old Testament is the verb "anah" which means to afflict, oppress, humble, be afflicted, be bowed down; to be depressed, be downcast; and be humiliated. Humility is the quality or condition of being <u>humble</u>. Humility in the Old Testament is the Hebrew word, "*anavah*" which means gentleness and meekness. Humility in the New Testament is the Greek word, "tapeinophrosynē" which is humbleness and lowliness of mind.

We can see the difference in man's definition and God's definition. God's definition of humble means to "afflict", "oppress", and "be humiliated". How many of us can say that we have been and allowed God to afflict us? Who has willingly been oppressed? Who has willingly been humiliated? Now, if we look at the definition from a Biblical standpoint, we can see that "humility" in the Bible has to do with the mind. Now, which of us can see a mind? Are you a mind reader? Have you been privy to see inside someone else's mind when you determine that one does not operate in humility? If your own mind needs to be washed by the water of the word, how can you determine what someone else needs to do with their mind? I have heard "Christians" say that someone has pride in their heart. Well, I understand that out of the abundance of the heart, the mouth speaketh. But how can you effectively analyze someone's heart when your own heart is deceitfully wicked (Jeremiah 17:9)? Oh! I love this one, I have discerned that he or she has pride in their heart. Do we understand that discernment is relative to spirits? When we speak of humility and being humble it counts when it is before the Lord. I have found deliverance in knowing that God is the only one that can see my heart, intent, and true motive. God does not give another person the ability to see "your heart". Only God, can see the "truth" of a heart.

The Purpose of Humility

Humility is designed by a loving God to produce the fruit of righteousness in our lives. This fruit of righteousness is so powerful when it comes in full bloom. God can look at us and see Himself. Humility determines your altitude in God. The more you exhibit humility, the more God can use you. Humility is likened unto brokenness. To some, brokenness is a curse word. Brokenness hurts! Brokenness means to be broken. Think of it this way, you take a glass and drop it on the floor; then it is usable. That makes no sense to a rational thinking person. But to God, he is probably thinking, what took you so long, now you are ready for my purpose. We are not truly usable until we are broken and unrecognizable. The best way to explain this is through the parable of the potter and clay. Jeremiah 18:1-6 contends, "The word which came to Jeremiah from the LORD, saying, Arise, and go down to the potter's house, and there I will cause thee to hear my words. Then I went down to the potter's house, and behold, he wrought a work on the wheels. And the vessel that he made of clay was marred in the hand of the potter: so he made it again another vessel, as seemed good to the potter to make it. Then the word of the LORD came to me, saying, house of Israel, cannot I do with you as this potter? saith the LORD. Behold, as the clay is in the potter's hand, so are ye in mine hand, O house of Israel." God cannot use us the way we were born, developed, and matured into adulthood. God must recreate us, so we are usable for His kingdom.

For God to recreate us, we have to be broken or as I like to say "destroyed". It is this brokenness that produces humility. The potter does not force the re-creation, he asks for permission. Interestingly enough, God will only use us if we allow Him. For God to use you, you need to welcome the brokenness.

The first step is to be thrown onto the potter's wheel. Thrown? Yes! I have actually watched the process of the potter. The clay was thrown onto a wheel and if it fell off it was thrown back. If it was not right, it was reconfigured and thrown again. Amazingly, God used this parable to show us what He wants to do with us. God is a gentleman. God asks if He can throw you, squeeze you, break you and expose you to heat and harsh elements. The end result is amazingly beautiful. The process will feel like death; the intent is to "kill" the old you. You cannot fulfill the purpose that God has prepared for your life without Him. You will fail miserably. Going through the tunnel of humility, places you in an honorable position. To truly be used by God, we must pass through the school of humiliation. Unfortunately, most withdraw before the perfect work of God is completed. Many of us have been humiliated before, for something really stupid we did. I have so many times. Have you ever been humiliated, for the cause of Christ? Have you ever been afflicted for standing on the word of God? Have you ever been rejected or downcast for obeying God? Better yet, have you been humiliated willingly? I do not know a lot of people that will say, "Bring on the humiliation."

Humiliation produces some awful feelings: embarrassment, hurt, feelings of hopelessness, despair, and grief. Thankfully, the beautiful thing is the feelings will pass. How will you operate in the midst of the humility? Will you quit? Or will you say, nevertheless thy will, O Lord.

The process God uses to produce humility, exposes the real intent of our hearts. Humility tests your obedience to God's commandments when pressure is applied. The production of humility is like an old-fashioned olive press. The olive press "crushed" the olive until oil was produced. The process of humility will "crush" you until the "oil" of God's anointing is pressed out in your life, (the words of Bishop T.D. Jakes). Whether God takes you through the potter's process or the olive press, the purpose is to "crush" you so that the oil He has placed inside of you can come forth. It is the "what's left" that God will use! He is never concerned about the "what was". God cares about "what's left". Humility ushers us into the "what's left" stage. I know crushing, is not appealing. I certainly can do without it. Crushing is a prerequisite for purpose. If you fail this part, you will repeat until you pass. You cannot handle the "honor" God will bestow if you cannot handle the pressure required to maintain the honor. There is no easy way. Humility is required.

I used to hear people say, you do not want God to humble you. I have learned and now understand that when God humbles you by the way of the wilderness, it is good. The "old folks" used to say you do not want God to "whip" you. But even if God "whips" you, it is for your good. Being disciplined by God, means we are His children. What we do not want is to experience the wrath of God. I am maturing in God; I am better able to handle "whipping" I know it is for my good. All things work together, for the good of them that love Him and are called according to "His Purpose" (Romans 8:28). Be not afraid, humility is good for you even if it does not feel good. Humility produces amazing fruits of righteousness. There is no other way to produce it. Welcome it. No, I am not crazy. It will bring out the best God sees in you.

No False Humility Allowed

It really takes my husband to talk about this. False humility is where many Christians hide. False humility is where Christians throw stones and hide their hands. False humility allows you to look at your brother and sister and boldly declare the pride in their lives. Because God showed you. Really? I mean, really? It is the place where one can say, I do not need recognition because I know who I am. Really, then why did you just say you do not need recognition? False humility is literally "counterfeit" humility. You almost need a microscope to see it. False humility is exposed in the presence of God. As a Bible teacher, I have found that if God is always "showing" you someone else; you can never see yourself. Either you are not praying to God or there is a "tinge" of flesh operating. Worse, you are wise in your own eyes. This is "pride". God never designed us to look at our brother and sister and analyze their walk. Leaders are charged to teach and preach the gospel. God never called us to be "Christian police". Pride makes us measure others. Pride is also in "false humility". It is liberating to know that no one can whip me with the "pride" stick anymore. Most of us will be working to eradicate pride until Jesus returns. Contradictory? We go from faith to faith; God reveals what we are able to handle. When we get victory in one area of pride, he shows us another area and the process continues. Since God hates pride, He reveals it to us, so He can create in us a clean heart. We should always be on guard. Our adversary, the devil is a roaring lion, he wants to devour us. He loves to devour those that "have it altogether". I admit, I am a work in "process" and "progress". False humility is not allowed. It is dishonest but God is truth!

I have great respect for people, who admit mistakes and try to make it right. When you blow it and are humble enough to admit it, then you may not struggle with false humility. Real saved people, struggle with saying, "I blew it". It makes them look like they missed the mark. That is why God lets us blow it, so we will know we need His grace and the power of His spirit. My husband defines "false humility" as appearing humble, but inside very prideful. It reminds me of a childhood story. There was a little boy, jumping up and down in the car and his mother asked him to sit down repeatedly. Then finally, she told him if you do not sit down, you will get a spanking. The little boy sat down, but he said to himself, "But, I am still standing up!" We must be careful. We can be prideful without realizing it. God is such a merciful Father. When we seek Him with all of our heart; He will show us our transgressions and give us the opportunity to repent. Thank God!

Repentance allows humility to be demonstrated in our lives. False humility will die as we journey through process. False humility can cause detours and U-turns. Purpose is a forward process and the absence of humility will abort the process if left unchecked. We check "false humility" through prayer. When I go to God about the "sin" in someone's life, the first sin He discusses is mine! We should pray for others deliverance, but with right motives. God is good, He will not let us bypass Him, trying to correct someone else. Can't you just see us, saying God, "They have this problem? They did this to me God, and they need to do this and that God." God is saying to us, if we are listening, "You did this, what about when you did that, and you need to do this." God is a relational God; He is concerned about your pride more than your brother's pride.

The Wilderness

In *Dangerous Surrender*, Kay Warren talks about the "Kingdom of Me". The "Kingdom of Me" is where everything is about you, for you and just you. No need to worry, everyone has a "Kingdom of Me". Your kingdom just has not been invaded and demolished like the walls of Jericho. Yet! The wilderness helps make those walls fall flat! Can the wilderness be that powerful? If you stay in it long enough. It can suck the very life out of you, and it should. It is designed to "kill" you, but you must not die there. It is supposed to be temporary. It will feel like forever, but I promise it is seasonal. You determine how long you stay! I found out, how to get out. A wilderness is a wild uncultivated region, uninhabited or inhabited only by wild animals. It is interesting that a wilderness is either uninhabitable or inhabited by wild animals. Hmm? Are we like wild animals when we refuse to surrender to the plan of God? Are we like a mule, stubbornly rejecting God? He has to throw us in a desert, for us to thirst for His living water. Or did He send us there so we could appreciate the Promised Land? In a desert, only certain types of plants and animals can live. We are not designed to live in the desert naturally and certainly not spiritually. The wilderness is for passing through. Wilderness in scripture, is the Hebrew word, "midbar" which means a large pasture or uninhabited land. It can also mean mouth. Please God, do not let our mouths be a wilderness. I believe this is what kept the children of Israel there forty years. Their mouth of wilderness!

God's Purpose for the Wilderness

If you are like me and went to church growing up, you heard about the children of Israel in the wilderness. You heard they were there forty years and some of them died because they murmured and complained. As a child, I knew I never wanted to go to the wilderness! Never! As I have matured in my knowledge of God, His Word and experienced my own wilderness, I learned something. There is beauty in the wilderness. What? Beauty? Beauty is experienced if and only if, we embrace the experience and God's purpose is fulfilled. God discloses His purpose for wilderness in Deuteronomy 8:2-3, "And thou shalt remember all the way which the LORD thy God led thee these forty years in the wilderness, to humble thee, and to prove thee, to know what was in thine heart, whether thou wouldest keep his commandments, or no. And he humbled thee, and suffered thee to hunger, and fed thee with manna, which thou knewest not, neither did thy fathers know; that he might make thee know that man doth not live by bread only, but by every word that proceedeth out of the mouth of the LORD doth man live." God's purpose for the wilderness is to humble us, prove us, to know our hearts and to determine our obedience to Him. He allows us to suffer hunger and need, so He alone can feed us. He wants us to know that we cannot live on (food) alone, we need the Word of God to live. It is love in its purest form. It is our experiences in the wilderness that makes God seem unloving.

The journey through the wilderness for the children of Israel was supposed to be a short journey. It took forty years for God to work His purpose. It took forty years because of their complaining, murmuring and disobedience. These "three" things can prolong our journey in the wilderness. Although, the wilderness was a desert with extreme conditions that should have caused desolation and defeat, they were sustained. God says in Deuteronomy 8:16, "Who fed thee in the wilderness with manna, which thy fathers knew not, that he might humble thee, and that he might prove thee, to do the good at the latter end." Wow! The wilderness is designed for good at the end. Most never endure to the end because we are engulfed by the surroundings of the wilderness. God uses the wilderness to humble us or dethrone us from the control of our life. It is not our life and we cannot do what we want to do. When we ask God to save us, at that moment, we give up control of our life. So, why do we act like God has done us an injustice when we pass through the wilderness? Our spiritual ancestors went through the wilderness. Some of the prophets went through the wilderness. John the Baptist was a voice crying out in the wilderness. Jesus was led to the wilderness to be tempted.

If everyone before us went, guess what, we are going! The wilderness is inevitable in the life of the believer. It is essential for purpose. The wilderness humbles us first, by rendering us powerless. There will be things that will happen in the wilderness that you cannot fix, finagle, negotiate, reason, wrestle or understand. You have to come to the end of yourself and just let it happen. Everything you do to fix it, will make it worse. Humility will make you throw up your hands and say "Okay, God you win." The chain of events in the wilderness will let you know it is God; the devil will get no credit for this "character-building" exercise. You will know it is God, His voice will be very clear. He will speak to you every step of the way, as your kingdom falls. He will affirm you with every brick that crumbles to the ground!

God will prove thee in the wilderness. The word "prove" means to test. God uses the wilderness to "test" what is in you. The Hebrew word for prove is "nacah" which means to test or put to test. This is where God shows you who you really are. He already knows because He created you. Are you a faithful or fearful witness? Honestly, cowards will die in the wilderness. The wilderness is not for the fearful. The level of testing in the wilderness can cause anxiety, stress, and restlessness. If your faith is weak you might have a heart attack, a mental breakdown or worse you will lose faith in God. These tests will determine if you will pray or pout. To be honest, you might pout, I did. I discovered my pouting did not do much. It did eventually lead me to pray, pray and pray some more. I saw more results from prayer than I did from pouting. As a result, prayer was established as law in my life. Do not misunderstand me, I prayed before. I had a prayer life, but my prayer life skyrocketed. This proving will determine if you will shake your fist at God. You might. I did. God is so merciful. I am certain of one thing, if no one loves me, God does.

He will prove you to see if you will cry out in pain or cry out in faith. I did both, God comforted. He will prove you to see if you will lean to your own understanding, or will you trust Him. The more I tried to do things my way, the wilderness just slapped me around. I said again, "Okay, God you win". God will prove you to see if you will give up. Or will you say, "Nevertheless thy will!" I felt like giving up. God was pruning me. I began to say, God it does not matter how it looks, I trust you. There were days, with tears in my eyes, that I said, "Nevertheless, thy will be done." God will prove you to determine if you will succumb to fear or will your faith rise to the occasion. I battled with fear. I was afraid that God might not show up. But, after much proving, my faith did rise. Rest assured, there are no magic tricks or special strategies available in the wilderness. You pray, praise, cry if you need to, but you must "trust" God when you cannot "trace" God. God wants you to know your own heart. The wilderness is a discerner of the heart. It does the same work that the Word of God does in Hebrews 4:12. The very essence of the wilderness, places you between a rock and a hard place. You will either break or bail! Your "will" will be broken or you will give God the peace sign and forfeit your promise. The wilderness is not for cowards. I used to think it was not for children. But if you enter as a child, you will exit a fully, mature, fearless, and faithful believer.

The wilderness will test your belief in the authority of God's word. It will seem like your faith-filled words are powerless. The more you speak healing in the wilderness, the more the sickness and pain may be present. The more you declare the workings of Jehovah-Jireh, the more financially strapped you will become. The more you declare, He is faithful, the more it will appear that God is a liar. You might feel like God is deaf to your groaning because fear is in one ear and doubt in the other. Calamity may pay you a visit. Tragedy might call you on the phone. Suffering might sleep in the bed next to you. These wilderness inhabitants will ask, "Where is your God?" You must reply in faith. Can God trust you to obey at all costs? Can you still pursue His purpose if you are rejected, lied on, abandoned, and endure your name being scandalized? Your answers and attitude will decide the length of your journey. Will you say yes, when all your circumstances are calling you an idiot? God will use the wilderness to ask you, "Who do you say that I am?"

Israel's Wilderness

God performs great miracles through, around, in and with us through the wilderness experience. After the exodus from Egypt, the parting of the Red Sea and the demolition of Pharaoh's army, the children of Israel entered into the wilderness of Shur. In Exodus 15:22-27, the children of Israel were able to see the first of many miracles as they journeyed through their wilderness. In the wilderness of Shur, the waters were not suitable to drink. Like spoiled children, accustomed to slavery, having basic needs provided they whined about the water. Instead of asking politely, the children of Israel murmured against Moses. Moses cried out to God and the Lord provided instructions to purify the water. You would think the children of Israel would know God's character after all the miracles they saw in their exodus from Egypt. God made promises to Moses and the children of Israel predicated upon their obedience to Him. God tells them if they will consistently listen to His voice, do what is right in His sight, listen to His commandments and obey, He will keep them walking in healing. God kept His promises, and he gave them wells of water and palm trees to rest by. God provided stability in the wilderness. Have you ever seen wells of water or palms trees in the desert?

The children of Israel sojourned through the wilderness of Sin. Notice the name of this wilderness. It has been said that they journeyed through several wildernesses before they actually made it to the Promised Land. I believe, we visit certain parts of wilderness terrain for God to deal with the deepest parts of our souls. In Exodus 16, the children of Israel really got in trouble with God about their "wilderness" of the mouth. The children of Israel murmured and complained big time. Yet God, was merciful to them. They complained about the lack of food, questioned God's provision, and accused Him of leading them there to die. God tells Moses that He would provide bread (manna) from Heaven. God promised to only give daily bread. God used this to test their obedience and trust. In Exodus 16:4, "Then said the LORD unto Moses, Behold, I will rain bread from heaven for you; and the people shall go out and gather a certain rate every day, that I may prove them, whether they will walk in my law, or no."

Have you ever stopped to think that God limits our resources to see if we will trust in man's resources, or lie and steal to get what we "think" we need? Remember, God uses the wilderness to prove us. God provided for the children of Israel's daily sufficiency. Those who obeyed had no lack, nor abundance. Those who leaned to their own understanding and tried to get more than needed, their manna bred worms and rotted. When God is proving you through the wilderness, deviation from His instructions will end in shipwreck. You will be embarrassed and hopeless because you tried to circumvent God. They ate manna for forty years and kept some as a memorial to remind them of God's provision. We should record what God does in our wilderness; it can serve as a testimony for others. It amazed me that each time the children of Israel encountered a problem in the wilderness, God answered despite their murmuring.

Many people believe that God's mercy will run out. It is just not true. God will discipline us. He ended their murmuring, bickering, and complaining. God called them an evil congregation and judged them. We must be careful of our responses to our experiences in the wilderness. Wrong responses prolong the journey. There is power in our tongue, we can speak death to our promises and ourselves. Rebellion, disobedience and complaints from Moses and the children of Israel caused an entire generation to abort their promise. Believe it or not, your journey in the wilderness is a generational experience. You can determine generational blessings in your family. Moses' refusal to speak to the rock and his frustration with God's people cost him the Promise Land. He had to anoint Joshua, his replacement. Wow, can you imagine because you failed to do it God's way, God allows you to see and train your replacement? Your replacement could be your children. Everyone from age twenty and up died in the wilderness because of their unbelief and their continuous complaining.

Joshua and Caleb were the only two allowed to enter the Promised Land. They entered because they kept pure hearts and right responses. Joshua was appointed by God to lead Israel into the Promised Land. In the midst of wilderness, God is always preparing someone to lead in the fulfillment of His promises. It is dependent on their obedience to God. I always ask God to help me, so I will not become like the children of Israel. I do not want to prolong a short wilderness into a lifetime encounter. The children of Israel were supposed to be in the wilderness eleven days. They extended it forty years. The route to promise is always shorter in God's eyes. We see through a glass darkly and we frustrate the process through complaining, murmuring and disobedience. The wilderness is supposed to break our will. Allow the breaking, it is restructuring and very necessary.

Jesus' Wilderness

Jesus' wilderness experience was forty days. In Luke 4:1-15, Luke describes Jesus' experience. Undoubtedly, Jesus went through a wilderness experience very different from the children of Israel. The children were led into the wilderness by God to be humbled, proved and to secure their obedience. Jesus' wilderness experience served a ministerial purpose. The wilderness also prepares you for ministry. The wilderness for ministry equips you to become victorious over all the devices of the devil. Jesus was led into the wilderness directly by the Spirit of God to be tempted by the devil. Adam and Eve showed us, we are no match for the temptation of the devil alone. We need the power of the Holy Spirit to help us.

Jesus was led by the Spirit into the wilderness, was tempted for forty days while fasting. **Imagine that.** In Chapter 2, we talked about fasting. Most of us, if tempted while fasting would have caved long before the cock crowed. The first temptation Satan threw at Jesus was food. We know that fasting means abstaining from food, how ironic that Satan tempted Jesus with food. Satan told Jesus to command the stones to be made bread. Jesus responded with the Word of God, "It is written, that man shall not live by bread alone, but by every word of God (Luke 4:4)." Jesus was tempted with riches; many of us fail the test of riches. We desire the riches of the world more than the kingdom of God. Satan showed Jesus all the kingdoms of the world and all the power he would have. Again, Jesus responded with the word, "Get thee behind me, Satan: for it is written, thou shalt worship the Lord thy God, and only Him shall thy serve." Jesus passed the test of riches.

Jesus was tested with prestige and power, "the test of who you are." Many of us fall weak to this test. When you know who you are there is no need to prove it. The devil takes Jesus to Jerusalem, sets him on a pinnacle and tells him that because He is the Son of God, he could jump, and the angels would catch him. Not only was Jesus tempted with prestige and power, but Satan also misquoted God, like he did in the Garden. Jesus responded, It is said, Thou shalt not tempt the Lord thy God (Luke 4:12). The devil's schemes failed, and he departed for a season.

When you pass the wilderness exams, the enemy will leave for a season. He will return. Jesus, after the temptation, was endued with power. When you overcome the devil's temptation, you will receive Holy Spirit power. Once God humbles, proves, tries your heart, test your obedience for compliance, then and only then are ready for the test of anointing. The anointing to operate in purpose is born in the wilderness. In the wilderness, the enemy of your soul will test you like he tested Jesus. When you pass, you will experience the power and presence of God like never before. You will become a more effective witness for God, more effective in ministry and you overcome the power of the enemy. Prepare to pass the test because you will be promoted!

The Entrance to Purpose

Entrances have front doors. The wilderness produces humility and humility is before honor. Humility is the entrance to what God has planned. In Isaiah 43:19, "Behold, I will do a new thing; now it shall spring forth; shall ye not know it? I will even make a way in the wilderness, and rivers in the desert." In the wilderness, exits will be invisible and often there is an absence of resources and seemingly the absence of God's presence. God will make a way in the wilderness. In the wilderness, the children of Israel saw many miracles. Think of it in these terms, you must journey from your past, walk through wilderness, embrace humility, and then entrance to purpose! Just that simple! If you embrace humility through wilderness, promise is next.

There are some precious reminders that you need to keep for your testimony: unexplainable provision, feeling the abiding presence of God, purification of your heart, fearless faith, radical obedience to God and unmerited blessing.

Humility in the wilderness will lead you to purpose. In your purpose is fullness of joy, abiding peace and blessings overflowing with milk and honey. Wilderness positions you for purpose. You can only go through the front entrance of your purpose. You can try the back doors or windows, but they will not open. Humility helps you to remember that promotion comes from God. All victory is through Him. Fulfilling the purpose of God is an honor never a guaranteed place. There are preparations required for purpose and promise. Enduring the process of prayer, fasting, purification, separation, obedience, studying the word, hearing the voice of God, and humbling yourself before God will properly position you. You cannot bypass any of these processes. Completing each process will release certain keys that will unlock the doors of your purpose. Each process conditions you to willingly embrace humility. Proverbs 15:33 declares, "The fear of the LORD is the instruction of wisdom; and before honour is humility." If you desire honor, humble yourself. No humility, no honor! No humility, no purpose! No process, no pain. No pain, no purpose! The process gets you in the hallway, wilderness get you the power, but humility gets you the keys.

CHAPTER 10

∽◦∾

FORGIVING GOD

"Blessed is anyone who does not stumble on account of me"
Matthew 11:6

Forgiveness Defined

Most of us demand forgiveness but are often unwilling to extend it. Forgiveness means to release from rightful punishment. Honestly, the process of forgiveness was the hardest for me. I thought obedience and humility were tough, but forgiveness really crumbled my kingdom. Real forgiveness and the fruit of forgiveness only occurs when death has fully worked in you. Facing the depravity of my own soul has been an incredible experience, I had to admit my own brokenness. Truthfully, either we choose forgiveness, or we live in a place of bitterness, hatred, envy, anger, and strife. Living life in this abyss of darkness, is not life. Forgiveness means to give up all claim on an account; to grant pardon and to cancel all indebtedness and liability.

It may seem quite "prideful" to say I need to forgive God. Wow! God is the one person many will not admit they have an offense against. We have all struggled at times with forgiving people who have wronged us or forgiving strangers who have violated us in some way. We have struggled with forgiving ourselves for failures and self-injurious behaviors. Worst of all, we have to forgive God for the things that He allowed in our lives that we did not appreciate. Some of us have to forgive God for allowing our worlds to be turned upside down by tragedy, calamity, loss, and suffering.

Facing Unforgiveness

I remember the day I heard the Holy Spirit minister these words, "You need to forgive God". It seems foreign to say we need to forgive God. In actuality, many people that we encounter daily are really mad at God. I mean really mad at God! Honestly, there are Christians that need to forgive God for what He allowed and for what He did not allow. I would be lying if I said, I was never angry at God. I was angry for the some of the things that have transpired in my life, especially during process. But through the process of time, I have learned that what it takes to forgive others for hurt and offense can apply to God.

Beginning the Process

If you are expecting a twelve-step program to jump start the process, I do not have one. I will share with you what I know works. These strategies have withstood the test of time and are recorded in the Bible. The process of forgiving God begins when two things happen: incredible honesty and sheer nakedness before a Holy God. The difference between forgiving people and God is simply this, you can hide your emotions from people, but not God. He is always there, hiding is irrational. Jeremiah 17:10 contends "I, the Lord, search the heart, I try the reins, even to give every man according to his own ways, and according to the fruit of his doing." It does not take rocket science to recognize the fruit of unforgiveness: bitterness, anger, wrath, rage, disobedience and even death. It is unfortunate, that all of this is linked to our responses toward God's decisions. Incredible honesty means coming to God and communicating how you feel. He already knows. Being able to come to God, about issues in your life is humility, rather than pride. This level of humility can test the fiber of your being. It can shake the foundation of your belief system.

Job experienced incredible suffering and he inquired of the Lord. God responded to Job, not as he hoped. But God responded, nonetheless. It is heresy to instruct people not to question God. There are provisions in the pages of scripture that permit us to seek God for wisdom and understanding. I had to come to God for real and pour out my heart. I had to confess my anger about what He allowed regardless of my obedience to His will. I did not understand why obedience to God incurred such incredible costs. I confessed to God my pain from the persecution from family, that really hurt. ***Really hurt***. The separation from lifelong friends, character assassination, and slander from the church that I had given my life to serve, **really, really hurt**. I repented for rejecting the call on my life, despising God's instructions and being willfully disobedient.

Nakedness

Coming to God broken and in humility, then and only then, did the mask, the clothes, and the layers of religion peel away. I saw the depravity of my own soul that hurled powerful putrid accusations at God, "How dare you ruin my life? "I am good, I have done right!" "How dare you do this to me?" God could have struck me down, but His lovingkindness and righteousness allowed me to see my own self-righteousness, nakedness, and the need of a Savior. Naked before God, is being in the midst of the Garden of

Eden, eating of the forbidden and hearing God call your name with the evidence around your mouth. When God calls us, we are silent because we see how awful we look standing there nude. Nakedness before God always uncovers the pride, guilt, shame, and rejection we feel. Nakedness will uncover the intensity of the darkness embedded in our souls. It amazes me that we can be angry with God, the only one that can help us. God has covered our nakedness through the blood of Jesus Christ. I am grateful that His blood covers us. Our nakedness is required so we can be clothed in His righteousness.

Why Has Thou Forsaken Me?

"Eli, Eli, lama sabachthani? That is to say My God, My God, why has thou forsaken me?" Jesus uttered these words on Calvary's cross. Dying for the sins of the world, Jesus spoke these words in blood-dripping agony, while his hands were stretched beyond the sockets of his shoulder. His feet were nailed together by huge nails that exposed the bones in his body as they were hammered through. His head bleeding from the thorns being pushed in, all with the accusations and mockery from his accusers. The thorns caused blood to drip in His eyes, every piece of His body bruised and bloody, but not broken. This agony described in scripture and on the silver-screen pales in comparison to the suffering of our Lord. Yet, we cry, "Why God?"

Forsaken means to be deserted and abandoned. Jesus felt abandonment by God at Calvary, He became sin for us; and sin separates us from God. At times we can feel forsaken by God, although He promises He will never leave us or forsake us. "Let your conversation be without covetousness: and be content which such things as ye have; for he hath said, I will never leave thee, nor forsake thee (Hebrews 13:15)." These promises are throughout the Bible, but life can make us feel otherwise. Sometimes, we can pray and fast for healing and remain sick and in pain. We can pray for healing and wholeness for loved ones and they die. This often causes people to lose hope, deny the sovereignty of God, or worse… curse God and die (spiritually and physically).

I know you were hoping for an easy answer for such incredible dilemmas, there are none. Some things we will never be able to explain, that is why we call it "trust". I am learning to trust God when I cannot trace Him. When I feel abandoned because of unanswered prayers, I cling to the words of Job, "Behold I go forward but He is not there; and backward, but I cannot perceive Him; on the left hand, where He doth work, but I cannot behold him; he hideth himself on the right hand, that I cannot see him: But he knoweth the way that I take: when He has tried me, I shall come forth, as gold" (Job 23:10). If you are thinking, "that might work for you, but I do not have any more faith left in the promises of God", I am headed down your street.

We can cry out to God in agony for Him to help us and remain in our present condition. This place feels incredibly awful. This is a familiar place for me. Before I lost my house in foreclosure, I was lying on the floor crying out to God. And in the same moment, I was receiving nasty messages from a church member who left our church, who was also a very close family member. I thought God, "Are you kidding me?" as if I could not take anymore. I just knew angels were going to float into my room and minister to me like they did Jesus in the Garden of Gethsemane. They did not. There have been many times of crying out to God and it *seemed* He turned a deaf ear. I often use the word *seem*, because God promises that His ears are open unto our cries.

But Lord, I Obeyed You

Between the years of 2010-2017, I experienced incredible devastation, pain, agony, and grief, all while obeying the will of God for my life and ministry. Surely, God will not allow suffering when I am obeying Him? *Wrong again.* As believers, we have cheered and paraded around telling the whole world that we want to be like Jesus. We shout from the rooftops that we want to know Him intimately, but when He calls us to meet Him at Golgotha, we run like Jonah at top speed. Some of us even say, "No, Thanks Lord, I am good right here." Honestly, if I knew obeying God would cost me as much as it did, I would have gladly told God, See Ya! Obeying God has cost my life, yet I have seen God do some incredible, miraculous, and truly unbelievable things. It has been worth it.

During this part of the process, I got in big trouble with God. And it hurt like a paper cut on a pinky finger. This part left me neglected, ridiculed, lied on, and abandoned by family and friends. And to top it off, God asked me to pray for them and they were treating me like day old trash. The nerve! I definitely had every right to be mad, right? *Wrong again.* We are always asking God to make us more like Him and we mean it with our whole heart. We desire intense fellowship and we long to be in His presence. During these times, God taught me the real meaning of "the fellowship of His suffering." In Philippians 3:10-11, "That I may know him, the power of His resurrection, and the fellowship of his suffering, being made conformable unto His death: if by any means I might attain unto the resurrection of the dead." Whew! I read and believed this scripture for many years, but to live it, Lord Jesus. Let us face it, none of us think we deserve to die, but to live the life God promised, we must die. We must not forget, to live is Christ and to die is gain. Hmm. Dying means the end of all things, God calls it the beginning.

Many in Christendom have adopted a sinister superficial belief that obedience guarantees a trial free, hardship free and suffering free card. Not! Actually, the opposite is true, Hebrews 5:8 clearly shows us the cost of obedience. "He (Jesus) learned obedience through the things He suffered". I hated having to walk-out this scripture and learning the infallibility of the truth it declares. I pondered in my head, "Could I not learn obedience, just by being obedient?" Unfortunately, some obedience does not occur until the fruit of suffering has its perfect work in our lives. The journey of obedience has caused great suffering, mostly to the kingdom of ME and MY will. *Notice, how strong the 'me' and 'my' are.* Learning obedience through suffering helps erase pride out of our vocabulary, life, and heart.

The first test of radical obedience cost me "big" in the kingdom of me. Prior to this journey, I lived a very safe life, tried to make sure I never offended anyone, and if I did, I was quick to bring a peace offering (underlying man pleaser). I was so quick to make peace, even when speaking the truth of the gospel of Jesus Christ. Things that make you say, *hmmm.* As the bulldozer swung at the kingdom of me, I was climbing the education ladder professionally and financially very rapidly. God began to whisper to me, "I have need of thee." God asking for my resignation was not okay with me. I obeyed only after wrestling really hard with God. I typed my resignation later and took it to my boss, I surely did not expect what came next. I was ridiculed. I heard things like, "You are crazy, you are putting your career on the line." Family members said that "I lost my job" (shaking my head) because I thought

I was better than them. *Incredible*. Some spiritual mentors told me, "That is not God's will." "You need to work because you are in ministry and you guys need the money." I was more surprised by the "people of faith" responses' than anyone. I was in big trouble now. I looked like an idiot and a goody-two shoes. Uh oh! Now, I stared bone-crushing rejection in the face. How could people that loved me feel this way about me and tell me. Wow! I struggled to keep a pure heart and stay in a place of forgiveness. Frankly, I was mad and confused at the same time.

This shattered the walls of my self-image. This image that was shaped by my family, friends, church, profession, and my world. I was being conformed to the image of God. I was being transformed into who God created me, before I was in my mother womb. Just because it costs, and hurts does not mean you do not have to obey. The level of rejection was so intense. My former spiritual parents told me my life would not be blessed because they did not agree with God's plan for my life. Wow! I did not see that coming. Why would God instruct me to do something and the people who were supposed to be supportive, all but con-demned me to hell? I was completely annihilated. I had to decide to either keep peace, obey God, or run. I obeyed. I suffered behind that decision. Boy, did it come! With the support of my husband, I created By His Side Ministries. I have no regrets. I have seen ministry wives experience healing, salvation, deliverance, mar-riages healed and restored. The miracles have been incredible. I almost missed God because I feared rejection and ridicule. But God!

Family is very important to me. To experience family mem-bers who used to laugh and talk with me, suddenly could not stand to look at me. Whew! I endured being the object of ugly ac-

cusations and nasty looks as if I was the "pawn" of Satan. I cried
my eyes out many nights. I never knew my heart could hurt like
that. I tossed and turned at night for years. Good grief, it was
rough. I cannot pretend that I am a super Christian and rejoiced
in being persecuted for righteousness sake. I started festering re-
sentment against them. And boy, was it building toward God
slowly and subtly. When I knelt to pray, God would whisper,
"Bless them that curse you, pray for them that despitefully use
you." I was not trying to hear that.

The greatest annihilation to the Kingdom of Me, was when I
went to God in pain and agony. And God reminded me that, yes, I
had obeyed Him, but I had left the weightier matters undone, *law,
judgment, mercy, and faith.* Mercy screamed in my soul, like a child
being stuck with a needle at the pediatrician's office. What? Show
them mercy and they are treating me like trash. Pray for them
and they are ripping my name into shreds. Yes, I died and obeyed.
Not only was God working me over with forgiveness, but He was
teaching me the true meaning of 1 Corinthians 13. We use the
term "love" loosely and do not really understand it. God was
teaching me how to love for real! Not only was I experiencing
loss of relationships, loss of personal credibility, loss of possessions, respect; I was experiencing loss of the self that I had been
all my life.

God was asking me to come to the cross and die and declare,
"Father, forgive them for they know not what they do." These
words are so easy to quote for the self-righteous, but it is different
when we have to live it. My kingdom was being burned to the
ground. I ignorantly believed that because I had obeyed God certain things should not happen to me. God was teaching me the
truth of Matthew 13:21, "Yet he hath no root in himself, but du-

reth for a while: for when tribulation or persecution ariseth because of the word, by and by he is offended." I learned that tribulation and persecution are the result of the "truth" of God's word. God was teaching me how to live the scripture, I was becoming a living epistle. In 2 Corinthians 3:1-3, "Do we begin again to commend ourselves? Or need we, as some others, epistles of commendation to you, or letters of commendation from you? Ye are our epistle written in our hearts, known and read of all men: Forasmuch as ye manifestly declared to be an epistle of Christ ministered by us, written not with ink, but with the Spirit of the living God; not in tables of stone, but in fleshly tables of the heart." God used persecution, loss, slander, and "necessary" hell to conform me to the image of Jesus. All that we endure, if we endure, God will cause it all to work for our good (Romans 8:28).

Don't Get Offended

Offense is a nasty occurrence in the Body of Christ. Offense causes divisions, separations, church splits and church hurts resulting in an army of wounded, battered Christians. Offense weakens our witness for the Lord Jesus Christ. The Greek word for offense is "skandalos" which means a movable stick; a trigger of a trap; or a trap. Offense is an impediment, and it can cause us to fall. Offense can be a violation or belittling of a social or moral rule. My favorite definition "sin". With all of our rules and morals, it is impossible for offense not to occur. Jesus tells the disciples in Luke 17:1, "Then he said unto the disciples, it is impossible but that offenses would come: but woe unto him, through which they come." Uh oh! But scripture tells us how to handle offenses. If we follow scripture, we can handle offense and protect the integrity of Christ's Church.

Unfortunately, it is not clear on how to handle offenses directed at God. Yes, God! When God is walking us through process, and trial and tribulation occur, or we experience the chastening of the Lord, if we are not careful, we can become offended with God. We are self-righteous when we say when can never be offended by God. Do a heart check, there is some stuff in our hearts that would scare the pants off some people if God were to expose it.

If John the Baptist, the forerunner of Christ, struggled with offense, it is quite possible that you or I might walk down, "Offended by God Avenue." I parked and built a house on this street. And when I tried to move out, offense would suck me in like a Hoover vacuum. It took time to foreclose on my house on Offended by God Avenue. The foreclosure process on a house is quite lengthy and arduous. Every now and then, I am tempted to drive by my natural and spiritually foreclosed home. I stopped driving by my naturally foreclosed home because I had to let die what God allowed and trust Him. Spiritually, I have abandoned the house on Offended by God Avenue, so that I can embrace the blessings God has for me. Do not think the devil doesn't still try to entice me every once in a while.

John the Baptist was perfect and upright, obeyed all the rules and did exactly as commanded, yet he found himself in prison. Most of us do not even come close to the integrity and obedience of John. At best, we obey some of God's commands sometimes. Other times we are so engulfed in self-righteousness which keeps us from realizing that without grace we will never be what God has called us to be. Without grace, all the laws we obey, the righteous deeds we do and the wickedness of our heart that hides from us, we will never measure up. John was the epitome of what he preached, yet he found himself in a circumstance. John a man like us, I am sure pondered, "How did I get here? Am I not doing the work of Christ? Am I not obeying the will of God? Surely there must be another Christ? Or maybe I missed something? I chuckle every time I think about the times, I asked these questions. How many times have you asked the very same questions? How many times have you looked at your situation and wondered about the reality of God? The reality is, that even when you obey God some awful things can happen.

In Matthew Chapter 11, we get an opportunity to peak into the life of this committed prophet. John heard the conversations about Jesus. He heard about the miracles that were taking place. He must have pondered, "How can this be, and I am here?" John sent two of his disciples to inquire of Jesus. Matthew 11:3, "And he said unto him, Art thou the Christ, he that should come, or do we look for another?" Jesus told John's disciples to go and show John the things which they see and hear. More specifically, he tells John's disciples to tell John, "the blind receive their sight, and the lame walk, the lepers are cleansed, and the deaf hear, and the dead are raised up, and the poor have the gospel preached to them." This next verse was the key to John being delivered in his present circumstances, "And blessed is he, whosoever shall not be offended in me (Matthew 11:6). Wow! So, John finds himself in prison, Christ's deity is confirmed, and Jesus sends word that he is blessed if he does not get offended. Jesus did not address John's present circumstances. Christ confirmed John's calling and let him know the results of His calling. Then Jesus justifies John. God will never defy His own word. Romans 8:30, "Moreover, who He did predestinate, them he also called; and whom he called, then he also justified: and whom he justified, them he also glorified."

John was born to be the forerunner of Christ and all of his experiences were the result of his calling. God predestined John to be a voice crying in the wilderness. Jesus not only justified John, but He glorified John in death. John was glorified just as Jesus was on the cross.

John was beheaded for his calling, albeit, through lies and deceit. John's assignment and purpose was fulfilled. Although John did not know his purpose had ended. When Jesus learned of John's death, he departed to a desert place to restore himself. John was his cousin. John's life shows us there is blessing naturally and spiritually in death. The blessing will only come if we avoid offense. We lose the blessing when we take the "bait" of offense. Stay away from offense, it will cost you.

The Consequences of Offense

Offense is the "bait" that Satan uses to lure us away from God and rob us of our due season. The bait of offense is wicked and subtle, it powerfully wreaks havoc that can take years to repair. Satan always opposes the work of God; he is the accuser of the brethren. When we yield to offense, we play right into the clutches of Satan. He does not play fair; he will kick you when you are down. We can see the consequences of offense through the life of Job, no one suffered like Job. Satan tried to use the "bait" of offense through Job's wife to lure him away from God. Job's wife was so disgusted with the circumstances, she told her husband to curse God and die. She yielded to offense and forfeited the double-fold blessing when his "captivity" was turned. Offense is sin, it is sin against anyone. Offense at God, Lord have mercy!

When we experience incredible suffering, loss, tragedy, trial and persecution, Satan will present himself. *Inside strategy*: Expect him to do it, guard yourself with the sword of the Spirit, which is the word of God. It will work every time. Offense can take you into a dark place of despair if you allow it. Offenses can cause strife and bitterness. It can get ugly and nasty when directed at God. You need God to get through the incredible circumstances, yet you are mad at Him. I have been there. Satan knows if you do not allow offense to grip you, an awesome due season laced with double-fold blessings is waiting. This type of blessing punches holes in the kingdom of darkness, it serves notice that God's word is true, and He is faithful. Why do you think Satan works so hard to convince us that we are forsaken? Why do you think Satan tells us, that God does not care about us? When God tells us to cast our cares on Him, for He careth for us? Have you noticed that Satan tries with the bait of offense to get us to forfeit the promises in God's word? John Bevere, the author of the *Bait of Satan*, delves into how Satan master weaves offense. Offense is not our response to the situation; its origination is from the devil. If you take the "bait" of offense you will sign a death certificate. God provides for our life, peace, and eternal joy. Offense provides emotional battery and turmoil. Do not yield. Satan is selfish and jealous; he does not want us to experience the promises of God.

It's Not Fair, But God is Faithful

The beauty of God's faithfulness in the midst of devastating tests and trials, is God's favor. How is that possible? In the worst of circumstances, you can experience incredible supernatural favor. One of the patterns of God is, irrespective of your circumstances, God's word over your life will not return void. When Daniel found himself in the lion's den, he fixed his heart on God and the Lord's favor and faithfulness caused the mouths of the hungry lions to be shut. The presidents and princes were envious of the favor on Daniel's life and they sought to destroy Daniel. Daniel's obedience to God, caused God's favor to rest on his life. The accusations appeared to have succeeded when the king signed a ridiculous decree, that stated that if anyone bowed to anyone other than the king they would be thrown into the lion's den (Daniel 6:7). This decree complicated Daniel's life, but Daniel was committed to his God. Daniel prayed three times a day, fully aware of the ramifications of the decree. Daniel's loyalty to God convicted him to the lion's den. What a setup! Daniel was sentenced to the lion's den and a stone was placed to ensure he could not escape. The faithfulness of God prevailed. In Daniel 6:22-23, Daniel was found the next morning, unhurt and alive because he believed God. In my process, I witnessed the incredible faithfulness of God. Many times, I found myself in financial dens of no fault of my own. There were times I could not buy food, because there was no money. But I am a sower. I sow in tears, finances, prayers, encouragement, in the Spirit and in the word. Yet, I had no money to buy food for my family. One particular night, I had to teach Bible class, I prayed these words. "God, I do not know what you are doing, but I trust you to provide for my needs, Lord, it is on you." After Bible class, someone walked up to me and handed me an envelope. The words in the card blew my mind, "keep sowing"; and there was enough money to buy food. Wow! God was now teaching me how to receive from his hand. I was mad at God because I was used to making big $$$, and now I had to be fed like Elijah. Lion's dens are set-ups for God's favor and faithfulness. In the midst of unprecedented chaos, we forget God's faithfulness. God allows circumstances and situations to remind us that He is still God.

I learned of God's faithfulness as a young adult. My sophomore year in college, I had a car accident that left me owing a huge balance after the insurance paid out. Insurance companies can be robbers. As a student, I had no real job or money. My parents were certainly not in a position to help me. I had to lean and depend on God. The claims adjuster called to inform me, that I owed the insurance company $17,000.00. Where was I going to get $17,000.00? I told her that I did not have that kind of money. She said it would need to be paid but she would see what she could do. While I was on the phone with her, a song was playing in the background, "Be Encouraged." We ended the conversation and I went to the only place I could go and that was on my knees. I prayed like I had never prayed before in my life. While I was praying, the insurance adjuster called again. She told me that underwriting had reduced the bill from $17,000 to $1,700. Incredible, but I did not have $1,700.00 dollars. While I was explaining this to the adjuster, the song in the background was, "No weapon". When we ended the conversation, I got back on my knees and said, "God if you can do that, then I know you can wipe it out." The phone rang a third and final time, the insurance adjuster told me the debt had been cancelled. I was blown away, I nearly fainted. In difficult financial times, I remind myself of this. God wants to be believed. Even if we believe not, yet he abideth faithful, he cannot deny himself. When life is unfair, that does not change the faithfulness of God. It gives God an opportunity to show himself strong.

Prison Circumstances Can Produce Palace Promises

We have to forgive God for the circumstances that seem to imprison us. Unless we forgive, we will not inherit the promises that come as a result of the prison circumstances. When I think of prison circumstances, I am reminded of Joseph. Joseph's life is picturesque of promise, process, prison then promotion. Each stage of Joseph's life represents the process that many of us are in and will be promoted to if we trust God. We must resolve to not be offended by what the Lord allows. We must forgive God. My favorite definition of prison is "a place of execution". Prisons are activated in the life of a believer so we will "die" to the rudiments of this world. The rudiments of this world cannot stand in the presence of God, nor has any viability in His kingdom. The rudiments of this world will impede the promises of God in your life, they include philosophies, vain deceit, and traditions of men. If you are a believer and you find yourself in a place that feels like a prison, it is necessary. In prison your movement is restricted, it is a place of nothingness. By man's standards, it is a hopeless situation, but in God it leads to promise. Forgive God. Do not die in prison, you are almost there. The prison is designed to rid you of everything in your life that is in opposition to the plan of God. When we are unfamiliar with the promises of God, we call it our prison life. God must walk you through the prison, so He can be revealed. Joseph found himself in many prisons, it was God's plan and purpose. Joseph's life became a "living hell" after he received a word of promise from the Lord.

In Genesis 37, the Bible tells the story of Joseph. Joseph was favored by his father and God. The only problem was that his brothers hated him for it. Joseph has two incredible dreams about his future that included his family. But when Joseph told his family about his dreams, they had major problems with his dreams. His dreams caused his brothers to hate him more. Jacob, his father was careful in how he responded to Joseph. How about that? The people that are supposed to love you and be happy for you, despise and hate you. All you understand is that God has shown you His will for your life. God's purpose for Joseph's life necessitated him having the right leadership ability and the right heart. Joseph was blessed with riches, favor, and power but it was important that he not seek revenge later. Stop! Joseph endured incredible persecution from his family, he was thrown into prison by his brothers, and some of his brothers wanted him dead. These events alone were enough for Joseph to build hatred in his heart against his family.

Prison cells have the unique ability to expose everything in your life and heart that is unlike God. If you stay there long enough, all you will want to do is please God. Could it be that you have remained in your holding place because you are being conformed to the image of God? Sons move at their father's command. Most importantly, sons learn not to despise the spankings of the Lord (Proverbs 3:11-12). For the chastening brings forth wisdom and understanding that is more valuable than silver and gold. Lord, is there another way? Maybe. If you find yourself in a prison, your destiny with God is awesome and amazing. God must qualify you to handle the weight of the blessing. After Joseph was sold into slavery to the Ishmaelite, and brought to Egypt, his journey to the palace began. Joseph was sold to Potiphar, the captain of the prison. This must have been terrible for Joseph, rejected by his family, left in a pit in the wilderness to die, sold twice, and now he is in a country far from home.

I love this part, in Genesis 39:2, "And the Lord was with Joseph, and he was a prosperous man: and he was in the house of his master the Egyptian." How do you prosper in a prison as slave? Can you be blessed in the middle of the worst time in your life? If God has spoken a word over your life, His word is true from the beginning and no circumstance invalidates God. God's word concerning you must be tried but God protects, supports, and defends you when you trust Him (Psalms 119:160). Joseph was promoted in Potiphar's house, but Potiphar's wife found Joseph irresistible. Joseph maintained his integrity and faithfulness to God, and his refusal to given into the demands of Potiphar's wife, cost him his position in Potiphar's house. Joseph found himself in prison again. But the Lord was with Joseph, showed him mercy, gave him favor with the keeper of the prison, and Joseph rose to leadership again. Even in prison, God will bless you with incredible favor with people. If you do not get offended and forgive. God can bless you to do impossible things. I can assure you, there is favor even in prison.

When I married my husband, I was a deer in headlights. I was wondering, "How in the world am I supposed to be a minister's wife?" While in the Christian bookstore, I came across a life-saving resource, "A Handbook for Minister's Wives" by Dr. Dorothy Patterson. This book saved my life, my marriage, and our ministry. I had no clue that God was master weaving behind the scenes. I met the author in person, she was the guest speaker during one of our ministry wives retreat. We became wonderful friends. How awesome! God is always working on our behalf, even in the rough stuff. God has given me such favor with people, it baffles me. I have been richly blessed. The favor of God is priceless. **Forgive God.**

In prison, Joseph began to operate in his prophetic gifting and interpreted dreams. As a result, his gifting placed him two years closer to his promise. Joseph did not know this, but God did. It is astounding the revelation and wisdom that can be birthed in confined circumstances. What awesome things have God placed in you that you are refusing to do because of your circumstances? Be it known to you; this book was being written while in the midst of my greatest affliction. If you are in process, it is God's will for you to read this story. Could it be that you are so close to your breakthrough that if you obeyed God it could launch you right into destiny?

Joseph interpreted the dream of the baker and the chief butler. Joseph only had one request, that the chief butler remember him. Joseph remained in prison another two years. He had yet one more lesson to learn, promotion comes only from the Lord. Psalms 75:6-7, "For promotion cometh neither from the east, nor the west, nor from the south, But God is the judge: he putteth down one, and setteth up another." In the process of time, Joseph came to himself, and finally surrendered his heart and said, "Not my will, but Thine oh Lord". When the condition of Joseph's heart came into alignment with God's will, Pharaoh dreamed a dream. Pharaoh dreamed a dream that no one in his kingdom could interpret, except Joseph. Joseph's season for prison had expired and he was ready for promotion, (Genesis 41:9-13). In verse 16, we can see the maturity of Joseph, he met the qualifications for promotion. Joseph was promoted to second in command, he reported only to Pharaoh.

God does not halfway bring a promise to pass. He does it completely. In Genesis 45-47, we can see the fulfillment of the promise that God made to young Joseph. The keys to seeing the fulfillment of God's promises is full obedience, embracing process, forsaking all offense, especially with God. You must maintain your integrity, trusting fully in God and forgiving Him. If we take heed, like Joseph, we will experience, "And it came to pass."

It's Not Yours, Anyway

It is accountability time. We must all come to the place in ourselves where we realize we are not the absolute ruler and authority in the Kingdom of me. Your kingdom and God's kingdom can never co-exist. One of the kings must be dethroned. From my experience, it is pretty hard to compete with the King of kings. Competing with God, you will be mad, frustrated, weary and disgusted with life. We all believe that our lives, mates, children, homes, cars, quite frankly, whatever we pay for belongs to us. **Wrong**. The sooner we grasp this concept, the better. When we transfer our life back to God, life becomes easier to live. I have spent years trying to cultivate my life, and somewhere in the process, it got screwed up because I missed a step, or better yet, I became ooey, gooey possessive of my life. Truthfully, I did not want to fully obey God's leading. Try this on for size, God is the creator of the universe, the creator of me. My actions would tell God, His plans sucked. My actions literally said, "watch me and let me show you what is best for me." Hilarious!

We say this to God when we refuse to obey His leading. Okay, Mr. and Mrs. Rebellious, who knows better than God. I laugh or should I say kick myself for the time I have wasted, thinking I knew better than God. I realize that I know nothing, have nothing, and own nothing unless God allows. In Deuteronomy 10:14, "Behold, the heaven and the heaven of heavens is the Lord's thy

God, the earth also, with all that therein is." Everything belongs to God. This realization takes a minute to chew, longer to swallow and even longer to digest for us that are ooey-gooey possessive.

We have to learn to surrender the ownership of our lives, basically everything. Actually, a more suitable descriptor in God's grand scheme of things would be, "steward". A steward is a person who manages another's property or financial affairs. It took so long for me to get it; I mean really get this very simple principle. I laugh now, but for a couple of years, it was not very funny, especially when my life was turned upside down. I was hurting and other people were celebrating in my so-called calamity. To top it off, God asked me to bless these same people and forgive them. I thought, "Really God? Really God?" God meant **Really**!

God has blessed me with an incredible ability to teach and write. The problem with these awesome talents, I began to possess them like a baby with a pacifier. Trying to wean a baby from a pacifier can disrupt the lives of everyone in the house. I promised myself and God, if I ever have children again, they will *never* have a pacifier. Good Grief. I was the baby with the pacifier. Rather than commit my gifts and talents to the Lord for His kingdom and glory, I held onto them with a death grip. I knew deep inside, if I surrendered them to the Lord, I would have to die. I would no longer have control of my "gifts". After all, my "gifts" earned me position, prestige, and yes, power. Oh, how I loved being in control of me and my world. I sounded like Satan. Yes, Satan. "I" is Satan's favorite word. Actually, I did nothing in my life, God did it all and allowed me to participate. Everything I have, came from the heart and hand of God. In James 1:17, "Every good gift and every perfect gift is from above, and cometh down from the Father of lights, with whom is no variableness neither shadow of turning." So, all these "gifts" we think we have, they are not ours. They belong to the Lord.

When God asked me to "surrender" my gifts to the cross, I wanted zero to do with that. For years, I wrestled with God. He is such a merciful God, he still blessed some parts of my life, while the other parts were a mess. Several years ago, I pondered, "God there has got to be more than this". Everything was good, that was the problem; things were just good. Something was missing. Dangerous surrender was missing from my life. The Holy Spirit ministered to me these words once, "You do not mind doing my will, you just do not want to do it first." Years later, I would find these words prophetic. God's will must be first. He will never take second place, not to you, your dreams, your career, your marriage and certainly not your ministry. He must be first, or He will be nothing. To see God's purpose in our lives, we must bow "our stuff" to His sovereign will. We get mad when we have to embrace suffering, the loss of things, loved ones and friends. Our process infuriates us. Many of us are angry with God because we believe He is responsible for all the wrong in our lives. Quite frankly, until we keep company with Job, we have no business complaining about anything. Job loss all in one day, one day… and Job worshipped. Reflecting on the life of Job, I am embarrassed of the behavior that we as believers have exhibited when God desires to really bless us.

What? Bless? Yes, when we experience things like Job, there is another side, double. We often do not see double; we die in the process because we are mad at God. We curse Him with our tongues and with the way we live our lives. We will see the faithfulness of God, if we do not faint (Galatians 6:9, author emphasis). I have pondered once, while riding in my car, "God you allowed all this stuff to happen to me, my life." I really thought in my heart, "God why all these losses?" "God, Why?". A small still voice pierced the depths of my soul, "It's not yours, anyway!" Everything that I perceived I had lost never belonged to me. The gifts, that I did not want to surrender to God for the sake of the Kingdom, were not mine. What an incredible blow to my ego. So, if my stuff is not mine, I should not fight God when He asks for it. I would like to respond like Abraham when he offered up Isaac. Abraham knew God would not take something He promised, without providing something better, or without providing period. The things we give up for the cause of Christ, or the sake of the gospel, we will reap manifold returns. We qualify ourselves for the promise when we surrender for real. God knows when you truly surrender. **<u>You cannot fake surrender.</u>** It is a matter of the heart. The issue of surrender will stare you in the face, like brussel sprouts until you eat them.

Anything God asks us to surrender, know and understand that He did it first. He has a plan to bless you ridiculously! Your life, spouse, children, house and all your stuff, is not really yours. When you finally surrender, it is the greatest feeling of freedom. Don't be a pacifier-sucking baby. Your freedom depends on your surrender, so does your destiny!

The Power of Forgiving God

Forgiving God opens incredible doors. Forgiving God will open the floodgates in your life. Gates are a place of entry and exit. The Bible is full of prophetic examples of gates. It is hard to fathom that often our own actions stand between what God promised and the fulfillment of the promise. Forgiveness is huge with

God, so the lack thereof, can block, or even forfeit the promises of God. If unforgiveness is present, blessings, miracles, favor, and victory will be on hold, or absent. I am not sure about you, but I do not want to live my life frustrated, confused, and weary. I am ready for the floodgates.

In Matthew 18:15-17, it clearly explained how we should handle sin and offense with our brothers. Unfortunately, I have not found provisions on how to handle offense with God. The scriptures I read were about being careful not to be offended by God and that offenses would come. I am sure if you stay in offense and take Satan's bait you will quickly constipate your blessings. Constipation is not fun. If you have ever experienced constipation, then you understand the agony. Constipated blessings will haunt you if you allow unforgiveness to cycle through your heart.

Usually through process, praying and dying to ourselves, we can usually forgive people that hurt and offend us. Our thoughts before we forgive people remain inside and with God, hopefully. When we are mad at God, He can see it and hear it. We cannot hide from Him. Try this on for size, we are trying to command blessings according to Matthew 15:18-20, "Verily I say unto you, Whatsoever ye shall bind on earth shall be bound in heaven: and whatsoever ye shall loose on earth shall be loosed in heaven. Again, I say unto you, that if two of you shall agree on earth as touching anything that they shall ask, it shall be done for them of my Father which is in heaven. For where two or three are gathered together in my name, there am I in the midst of them," Our declarations just beat in the wind. Mmm. Are we sure our hearts are free from sin? Have you released God from fault for the things that happened in your childhood? Marriage? Finances? Church? Unanswered prayers? Until we forgive God, we block certain spiritual blessings in our lives.

When I found myself homeless, I was sitting on the couch at a friend's house, and my husband told me he wanted me to hear something. A preacher was delivering a message on forgiveness. He began to talk about all the people we need to forgive, but unfortunately, we had left out one person, God. God? I was so mad, I could have taken his computer and smashed it into a million pieces. God was the last person I wanted to hear about. I was in ministry, doing the will of God (not fully, unbeknown to me at the time), giving diligently to prayer, fasting, sowing in tears and everything in between. I was doing everything right and God let me be homeless. Why would God let this happen in front of everybody? People were laughing at us, talking about us, and having a party. Finally, I fell. I love God because all things work together for the good of them that love God and are called according to His purpose. God used the chains of this experience to deliver me from the concerns and opinions of people. He used it to deliver me from Mammon (demon of money and possessions), rejection, chains of my past and He used it to deliver me from the spirit of religion (a serious demon).

An all-powerful, all-knowing God used the hell in my life to bring me center point to His will. I got the greatest blessing and the greatest inheritance, I received Jesus himself. Through this process of forgiving God, He showed me who He really IS and what HE can really do. I had to forgive Him first. Before He could heal my marriage, before I could receive the blessings of men giving into my bosom pressed down shaken together and running over, I had to forgive Him. God has done so many incredible things. When I forgave God for real, I began to be flooded with the blessings. I am still witnessing the miracles God promised.

The Unlocking of Doors

Whenever I think of doors, I think of entrances and exits. I love doors that lead to things, but I struggle with doors that require exits. The doors that require exits have hard goodbyes attached. Good-byes are especially difficult. As God takes us through our processes, there are an array of doors that will be opened and closed. To handle these doors effectively, we must understand that if He opens a door, no one can close it (Thank God!), and if He closes a door, no one can open it (Oh Lord, but thankful now).

Learning the real meaning behind Revelation 3:7-8, has helped me manage the opening and closing of doors in my life. Revelation 3:7-8 decrees, "And to the angel of the church in Philadelphia write; These things saith he that is holy, he that is true, he that hath the key of David, he that openeth, and no man shutteth; and shutteth, and no man openeth; I know thy works: behold, I have set before thee an open door, and no man can shut it: for thou hast a little strength, and hast kept my word, and hast not denied my name." Open doors are God's choicest blessings for your life. Open doors are also a precursor for God to try the "reins of your heart". God knows everything, He wants us to know if we love Him more than what He can and will do for us. Open doors represent more opportunities for the sharing of the gospel, advancement of the Kingdom and being a blessing to others. Open doors are designed to bless you and your family. If your reason for asking God to open doors is selfish, they will remain closed.

We often perceive closed doors as punishment. We perceive closed doors as death to dreams and promises. We even perceive closed doors as "maybe I missed God", or "I have sinned". Closed doors are often opportunities for God to bless your socks off. Doors remain closed in our lives until we are prepared for what is awaiting on the other side. Closed doors are re-directives from God, to realign with His purpose and plan for our lives. Have you ever kicked a door until your feet were bloody and the door remain closed? Naturally, it is stupid to do so. Kicking a locked door does not open the door. It just hurts your foot. If you do not get mad and shift, you will experience double and destiny. Remember, the stuff behind the door is not yours anyway.

I have been an educator for many years. I have had incredible experiences in the field of education. Well, once God temporarily closed this door on me, thankfully not without notice. He told me He would close the door. I was livid because there was something required of me. Funny, people around me had "a different word from the Lord". I heard words like, "God closed this door because you think you are better than everyone, (family), God closed this door, because you are outside of His will (church members and other God-fearing Christians) and my favorite, God closed this door because He does not care how hard you have worked, and He does not care about you (Satan). Of course, when I heard all of these thoughts and voices it became pretty hard to hear God. God closed the doors in my life, so that He could shift me into the destiny He called me to, teaching in His kingdom. God desired to use the skills I had learned in Babylon to benefit the Body of Christ. How cool is that? Initially, I did not understand, especially amidst the chatter. *Sometimes, I still forget.* God, through closed doors began to teach me the sound of His voice. Closed doors ushers us to the cross, so we will be positioned for the promises of God.

Unforgiveness and disobedience will close doors that are supposed to be open to you. Deuteronomy 28 clearly details the blessings that are associated with a life of obedience. I was mad at God because certain things happened in my life. Well, after several years of tantrums, I discovered that I had left some things undone. The blessings are promised if you obey *all*, nothing lacking. I left parts of my obedience undone, delayed obedience is still disobedience. When God gives instructions, He expects them to be carried out fully and completely. The lack of fully and completely can cause "constipated" blessings. I hate any kind of constipation; I want nothing to do with my blessings being constipated. God's promises in Deuteronomy 28:12 says, "The Lord shall open unto thee His good treasure, the Heaven to give rain unto thy land in his season, and to bless all the work of thine hand; and thou shalt lend and not borrow." This promise is contingent on obedience to all that God commands. God requires forgiveness, it is a command. When we are mad at Him, Heaven will not rain. God wants to bless His children with more than we need or want to be blessed.

Well, how do we get the doors to open? We obey all of His words. When you have prayed for God to bless you, and you have done all that you know to do and there is still no rain, consider your ways. The prophet Haggai tells us to consider our ways in Haggai 1:3-12. The prophet Haggai presents a scenario or shall I say dilemma to the children of Israel and explains explicitly why there is a drought in their land. The children of Israel got the message and when they obeyed, the floods came, and their drought was demolished. There was severe drought during my process, there was an absence of what I know God had promised. I inquired of the Lord, "Why?" God in His infinite wisdom knew I was now ready to fully hear and obey His word. He breathed Deuteronomy 28:12 and 2 Chronicles 7:13-14 into my Spirit and the scales fell from my eyes. I through disobedience had caused 2 Chronicles 7:13 to come and reside in my house. I am called by God's name, therefore, I had to humble myself (surrender to His plan and His will for my life), pray (without ceasing, not asking for anything but devoting myself to Him), seek His face (Lord, what will you have me do?), and turn from my wicked ways (disobedience and unforgiveness) and then He heard me. I began to forgive God and really surrender to His plan. My skies became black like it did for Ahab when the prophet Elijah told him to go look again. I began to hear the sound of abundant rain, not only did I hear it, but Heaven also began to pour! Doors that are supposed to be open for you, will only open when you totally obey God. God always requires total obedience. You cannot disobey Him because what He requires makes you look incredibly stupid. You cannot disobey because you will be rejected.

The promises and blessings of God will far outweigh any loss. Obeying the principles of forgiveness generates blessings and the power of agreement will work. Some of the doors that have opened for me are so inconceivable, I get goose bumps just dwelling on the faithfulness of God. God will never share His glory with another. If you need closed doors to open in your life, consider your ways. We stand in between closed and opened doors. Why spend time swarming in anger, especially against God who has the power to catapult you from process to promise in the twinkling of an eye. It makes sense, His way, or no way. I like God's way; any other way is just dull.

Forgiving God Precedes Fresh Revelation

Meandering around the mountain of unforgiveness with God, is a long, brutal place. It can cause you to change your name to fit your circumstances. Some events are providential, often leaving us helpless and seemingly hopeless. In these moments, we must yield and discern that God is at work. If we are not careful and we yield to the "bait of offense" we become like Naomi in the book of Ruth.

Naomi experienced incredible loss. She lost her husband and both of her precious sons, and all that remained was her two daughter-in laws. The loss of a loved one is awful and definitely painful, and it becomes a real task to see blessing in the midst of incredible pain. Naomi became so stricken with grief and had such contempt for God, she no longer desired to be called by her God-given name. Naomi means "pleasant and delightful" she had deteriorated. In Ruth 1:20, "And she said unto Him; Call me not Naomi, call me Mara: for the Almighty hath dealt very bitterly with me." We can become so consumed with our circumstances that we direct blame toward the Almighty. We are the most pitiful at our pity party. We adopt the pity party theme song, "Woe is me!" I know this party ambiance too well.

Naomi's husband and sons' death required a change of direction for her life. She now faced a closed door. She succumbed to the closing of the door, as the Lord not loving her. She listened to the chatter of her circumstances. The chatter can at times drown out the voice of God. Naomi's chatter was so loud, she gazed at her circumstances more than God. Ruth 1:21, "I went out full, and the Lord has brought me home again empty; why then call ye me Naomi, seeing the Lord hath testified against me, and the Almighty afflicted me." Sound familiar? When we have been separated from all of our stuff and there is nothing left, save our lives and family, seeing and hearing God grows more difficult as time passes. Naomi could not see God's choicest blessing and what God was about to do with what she had left. In 1 Corinthians 3:13-14, "Every man's work shall be made manifest; for the day shall declare it, because it shall be revealed by fire; and the fire shall try every man's work of what sort it is, if a man's work abide which he hath built thereupon, he shall receive a reward." Naomi could not discern God's plan for her. She had no way of knowing except she trusted God. God had selected her to participate in the greatest miracle of all time. Naomi had a direct hand in connecting the two people who would be responsible for the birth of Jesus! What? God often uses our most devastating circumstances to create amazing miracles. Miracles are our portion, if we do not die in the process, stay out of offense, forgive God, and trust the process.

In the process of time, Naomi began to embrace the process of forgiveness with God. Through a chain of several events happening with her daughter in law Ruth, she was able to see the providence of God. Ruth 2:11-20 tells of the incredible story of Naomi, Ruth, and Boaz. Boaz was a very wealthy man who became interested in Ruth. Through this courtship, Naomi began to see that God was working even through her devastating loss. Naomi taught Ruth to prepare to for Boaz and the blessings of the Lord in her life. Through Naomi's words of wisdom, Ruth married Boaz and through their lineage came the Messiah.

Naomi thought God had dealt with her bitterly, but it was part of God's master plan. God, the master weaver, is always working good out of really rotten circumstances. God keeps His promises. You will not see the promise of God in your life if you cling to the sin of unforgiveness. Sin will cloud the vision of God's purpose in your life. God always provides fresh revelation and provision for His children.

If there is something missing in your life as a believer, dig deeper. God's word is true from the beginning. It is possible that you may just be in the way. Fully seeing the plan of God for our lives, requires using the tools God gives us. Obedience to His word will always unlock the purpose of God. If you walk in forgiveness, then you can command your blessings to be loosed. You will see what God has prepared for you. Naomi is a great example of what happens when we succumb to the circumstances of life, albeit allowed by God. She shows us what happens when we view God as the culprit and then when we see Him as the Creator. God desires to bless us; He desires for blessings to overtake us. He requires forgiveness.

CHAPTER 11

WALKING PROCESS OUT

"As a prisoner for the Lord, then, I urge you to live a life worthy of
the calling you have received."
Ephesians 4:1

Walking Defined

I have learned so much through watching my children. Learning to walk is one of the scariest times in the life of a toddler. Toddlers have to transition from crawling to the unchartered world of walking. It is funny to me that some children move from scooting to walking, never really crawling. Ironically, as sons and daughters of God we will do the same. Why is learning to walk so scary? First of all, you have never done this walking thing before. Babies move super-fast on the floor. They can travel at the speed of light and you will wonder what just zoomed passed you. When I was teaching my children to walk, I took their itty-bitty hands and held them up. Their tiny feet were in no position to move and their little legs were so wobbly that I had to tighten my grip. I had to position those little feet in a walking position, and I stood behind them as all "good mommies" do and guided each little step. I can picture their little slobbery grin as they approached their new season of life. Just as I guided my children in walking, there came a time, where I had to let them do it alone. I had to let them fall (my goodness, the horror!) so they would learn proper balance. I had to let them bump their heads on things, (heart-attack symptoms) so they would learn the safe places to walk and I cheered when they could do it with grace (each child was so different). Boy, was I glad they had learned to walk; it was getting tough trying to carry a purse, baby bags and a heavy child. God does the very same with us. When we first learn to walk, we are so unprepared. Our feet are crooked, legs wobble like spaghetti noodles and our hearts pound, as we take the first step. God knows that if we don't bump our heads, we will never learn His righteousness. If we do not fall, we will never learn His forgiveness. And when we fulfill His will, He is standing there cheering, clapping, and singing "Well, done." God never told us to run by faith, he told us to walk. It does not matter how scary; we just have to keep doing it.

Walk Off the Cliff

Early in my marriage, my husband's godmother told me, "Honey, trusting God is like closing your eyes and walking off a cliff." Her words proved prophetic. As I have matured in God, I have had so many cliff walking experiences. I needed a "spiritual insurance policy" to help cover all the seemingly broken dreams, hurt feelings, and disappointments. But those cliff-walking experiences have built fearless faith. In real life, I pretend to be a daredevil, but if I had to walk off a cliff, I am sure I would need to be resuscitated many times before I actually completed the task.

The closest I ever came to walking off a real cliff was during a leadership training exercise. Each semester, the leadership department was responsible for training educators for school supervisory roles. As part of the training, we had to attend an outdoor obstacle course. Really? It was more like putting your body through a paper shredder, and then putting the pieces back together, just before you were run over by a train. I had done pretty well, until it happened. We were all walking the trail discussing how insane the activities were, then my heart dropped to my toes, when I glared at the forty-foot high tree that I was supposed to climb, jump and catch a metal bar. I really wanted to damage the person that created this insane activity. There was no backing out for me, I was the leader of the group. I was mortified. My hands were sweating, my heart beating through my shirt, and my legs were shaking. Everything in me, said no, but my legs kept forward. I cried and prayed while climbing that tree, finally I made it to the top. I was deathly terrified at the top of the tree than the bottom. I stood there, waiting. Waiting to go back down, waiting to pass out, waiting to jump, just waiting. I took an eternal walk to the all-powerful metal bar and fear gripped my mind, heart, and soul. I repented for all the sins I had done up to that moment just in case something happened in the jump. I took a deep breath and I jumped. I missed the bar and dropped forty feet. I landed on my feet. I was alive and breathing. When they came to unhook the rope, they had to peel my fingers one by one from the rope and assure me that I was on the ground. Although, I could feel my feet on the ground. Everyone cheered as I walked away from the death grip, I cried. I am not sure if I cried because I was alive, or if I had just put my fear to the ultimate test. Either way, I was just glad to be on the ground.

Faith that becomes fearless is like that tree-climbing experience. There is a reason that God tells us, "Fear Not", because He knows that some tests will mortify us. God knows that we will experience fear as He leads us to the cliff. All of us will experience a cliff at some point in our walk. We can walk off bright-eyed and bushy tailed, or we can close our eyes so tight that our eyelashes leave imprints in our skin. It does not matter to God, what you do with your eyes as long as you do not let them guide you. We should walk with our faith, not with our eyes. When we have gone through all the processes, endured the pain, embraced the suffering, trusted God, then we come forth as gold. Gold is precious and not subject to corrosion. God knows that when He tries you in a certain area in your life, and you operate in faith, you will no longer be a target for the enemy. You become a weapon of mass destruction to the kingdom of darkness. God is preparing His people for unseen battles. God needs soldiers who can endure hardness and operate in faith. I heard for years; you should never be afraid of anything as a child of God. In theory, that is such a true statement. But in real life, some situations will scare the pants off of you. If you read the Bible, some of the most powerful men and women of God had their pants scared off, but they operated in faith and God's glory was magnified.

A Biblical Cliff-walk

King Jehoshaphat was the most powerful man in Jerusalem. As a king, you did not have to fight your own enemies; servants did it for you. Well, a day came when Jehoshaphat's faith in God was put to the ultimate test. In Chronicles 20:1-30, Jehoshaphat learned that the children of Ammon, Moab and others were prepared to take him out and all of Judah. The writers of 2 Chronicles, showed King Jehoshaphat's humanity and they showed his faith kicking in at the same time. We will experience human emotions when faced with scary situations, but your next response moves the hand of God. In 2 Chronicles 20:2-3 the Bible records,

"Then there came some that told Jehoshaphat, saying, There cometh a great multitude against thee from beyond the sea in this side of Syria; and, behold, they be in Hazazon-tamar, which is En-gedi. And Jehoshaphat feared, and set himself to seek the Lord, and proclaimed a fast throughout all Judah." We can see that Je-hoshaphat was afraid, but he responded in faith through fasting and prayer.

In an Ammonite and Moabite situation, the only thing left to do is seek the Lord. Everyone gathered together to seek the Lord's help. Often, when we get in a hopeless situation, we try to fix a God-sized problem with human wisdom. It will never work. The people of God came together to pray. Their prayer made the difference. They recognized God's sovereignty, they recognized their human frailty, reminded God of His covenant promise, and they asked God to recognize their inability to fight the battle. God responded. We have to get the formula right. God will respond to his word.

In 2 Chronicles 20:15-17, Jehoshaphat was afraid, but He responded in faith. That sounds ridiculous to most. When you are in a crisis, you pray and fast rather than freak out. It takes faith not to freak out, flip out or walk-out. Sometimes, you will see the greatest miracles when you are on the edge of the cliff. Where do you think Moses was standing when the Red Sea divided? In the case of Jehoshaphat, the Lord speaks, a beautiful site occurred. Every man, woman, child, including the king, bowed their faces to the ground and they worshipped God. **Imagine**. You are in trouble, you pray and fast, God sends a word, and everyone bows to the ground and worship. I love that the weapon that defeated their enemy was praise. They appointed singers to praise God. As they praised and worshipped the Lord, God set ambushments against their enemies. Their enemies killed each other. When the people of God came to look, they saw nothing but dead bodies. There was a bonus; riches lying among the slain. God gave them physical victory and they got bonuses that paid serious dividends.

In cliff-walking experiences, you can expect a no-way out situation, ugly ordeals and catastrophic events surrounding you, and there is nowhere to go but off the cliff. If you follow the will of God, He will catch you. The hardest thing to do is to stand still because something needs to be done and it looks like God is doing nothing. If we do what God said, believe what God said, He will set ambushments against your enemies. Trust Him.

Purpose-driven Walking

We need purpose-driven walking experiences to build fearless faith. You think the initial call is scary, wait until you start walking in your purpose. When God calls you, you might feel timid and unable to fulfill the call. But trust God. Obey. Walk into purpose – shaking but walk anyway. These purpose-driven walking experiences are designed to see if you trust God or your ability to fulfill purpose.

It takes faith to stand for righteousness even in the face of persecution and slander. These experiences create fearlessness, amid wickedness and really hot fire.

Fire-walking

Walking through fiery circumstances are deliberate and designed to align us with God's will. The fierier the walk, the more breaking occurs, the more surrendering to His will, the greater the blessing to be revealed. Most of us have never been thrown in the fire and lived to tell about it. Although, our trials and tests feel like an inferno. The three Hebrew boys were thrown into a fire, bound, chained, but fully dressed. They fell down into the fire. The men who threw them in were burnt to a crisp. In that fire, miraculous stuff happened. At least five miracles transpired in that fire. First, they were not smoking charcoal, they were alive. They were loosed from their chains. **Food for thought:** a blazing inferno will burn the chains that have you bound. Jesus showed up. Now, it amazes me that Jesus shows up out of time, because the children of God were in trouble. The most miraculous of all, their enemy, saw God.

King Nebuchadnezzar recognized the sovereignty of God. He made a decree that anyone who speaks falsely against God would be cut in pieces and erased off the face of the earth. Finally, the three Hebrew boys were promoted. Did you know that being baptized in fire promotes you? If you are in a scorching inferno, and obeying the voice of God, yielding to God your fear, promotion is next.

After You Have Done the Will of God

O Lord, how long shall I cry, and thou wilt not hear! These are the soul-panicking words of the prophet Habakkuk. How long must I endure this, O Lord? God, when are you going to deliver me? How long must I endure this sickness and suffering? These are the cries of God's people all around the world. Just like God answered Habakkuk in Chapter 2:2-4, "And the Lord answered me, Write the vision, and make it plain upon the tables, that he may run that readeth it. For the vision is yet for an appointed time, but at the end it shall speak, and not lie: though it tarry wait for it; because it will surely come, it will not tarry. Behold, his soul which is lifted up is not upright in him; but the just shall live by his faith." The key to this prophetic word to Habakkuk was God's appointed time.

What is God's answer to your cry for Him to show up? Hebrews 10:36-37, "For ye have need of patience, that, after ye done the will of God, ye might receive the promise. For yet a little while, and he that shall come will come, and will not tarry." God has an appointed time in which He delivers on promises. His promises are contingent on one thing, obedience. For those questions of when, where, and why O, Lord, the answer is the completion of God's will. Have you done all the God has asked? Is there any area of disobedience in your life? Have you completed the task fully?

Appointed Times

An appointed time for deliverance is when the appointed task is completed. God has made some promises to many of us and we are yet waiting. When God makes a promise, and gives you a time that he will deliver, He will deliver. As He did with Abraham, he will with you. God always has an appointed time. The only way you miss the appointment is through disobedience.

On July 28, 2010, I was praying, and God was calling me to full-time ministry. God spoke to my heart, "If you would be sold out to me, you will see the miracles that you read about." I wrote these words in my journal to keep track of God's promises to me. I keep a written record of God's faithfulness to me. A year later, On July 28, 2011, I was flying to Houston, Texas for a conference for pastors' wives. I did my normal routine of prayer for the pilot, flight attendants and every person on the plane. I began to read my book. Half-way through the flight, I became uneasy. The Lord spoke these words to my heart, "This plane is about to crash, intercede until I release you to stop." I had a window seat, and I did not see a need for prayer because everything appeared clear. I prayed against an unforeseen storm, my eyes were closed, and I prayed relentlessly. After praying for ten minutes or so, I opened my eyes to a very dark, thick, cloud outside of my window. This cloud looked scary. I continued to pray, I remember praying Mark 4:41, What manner of man is this, that even the winds and sea obey him? As the plane is going into this very dark cloud, the flight attendant walks down the aisle and begins to talk to the man behind me and mentions the word "wind shear". I asked, "What is a wind shear?" And she said, "It causes crashes." She did not know what God had spoken to me. I prayed and prayed, asking God for mercy.

The next twenty minutes of the flight were frightening. The pilot announced over the speaker, "We cannot land this plane." The storm will not give us clearance and we will have to fly in the air until we get clearance. With this news, I am still praying that God will command the storm to cease. A few minutes later, the pilot announces. "We are low on fuel and we cannot continue to fly in the air." The storm got really intense, I continued to pray the Word of God and remind God of His covenant with me. I asked God to remember the people and their families and the lives that would be impacted if this plane does not land safely. The pilot announced, "We will have to fly to San Antonio, to get gas because we are about to run out of fuel." I continued praying, surprisingly no fear. Then God speaks to me and says, "It is well". When He says, "It is well, I looked out my window and I watched the storm literally change directions. That was the most amazing thing that I have ever seen with my natural eyes.

Moments later the pilot announced, "We are cleared for landing." I had witnessed God calm a storm just as He did in the Bible. I can say, "What manner of man is this that even the wind, and sea obey him?" When we landed in the Houston airport, I was so happy to be on the ground, I gave God exuberant praise. I am sure people in the airport thought I was completely insane. I was thankful to be alive. I did not realize the magnitude of this miracle, until I got to the hotel and opened my journal and saw the date, one year earlier. Amazing! I saw a Biblical miracle happen in my own life. If God says something, He is faithful to perform it.

Double for Your Trouble

You will have double for your trouble, is a cliché. Until now, I never really understood the meaning. If you are reading this final chapter that means that I have completed the will of God for this season of my life. I have survived years of extreme difficulty. I have survived severe financial distress, sickness, and pain. The awesome thing about these financially devastating circumstances is that I witnessed God as Jehovah-Jireh. I have endured excruciating, chronic physical pain. There were days when I was in so much pain, I could not walk. I would have to crawl up my stairs just to get my children ready for school in the mornings or to clean. There were times that the pain would be so severe that all I could do was cry. I could not move, I had to just lay in pain, because I did not want to be addicted to painkillers. I have had two surgeries and I have healed beautifully. Hallelujah!

I survived severe persecution, people that I love have turned their backs on me, scandalized my name and attempted to destroy my character. I have forgiven them. Some relationships have been restored some have not. Either way, God has proved himself faithful. I purposed in my heart to please the Lord. The ultimate blow is to have the Body of Christ persecute you I thought, but when it comes from family, it is worse, and it can leave you so broken. God has used this brokenness to usher in salvation, healing, and deliverance to my family. When everyone walks away, God is enough. Persecution makes you sensitive to the needs of hurting people. I have embraced a new family concept, family are really those that do the will of God, the Father.

I survived my life being flipped upside down, turned inside out, and right–side up and I did not lose my praise. I love that. Sometimes, it was not as loud as I would have liked, because I was being broken. God was after the breaking. God is never after your job, career, finances, or relationships, He is after you. God wants you to come away with Him, fellowship with Him, that you may know Him. I learned who God is. He just is.

Isaiah 61:7 declares, "For your shame ye shall have the double; and for your confusion, they shall rejoice in their portion: therefore, in their land they shall possess the double; everlasting joy shall be unto them." It is so good to know that some clichés are true. When you eradicate all of your disobedience through obedience, God fulfills the double-fold promises.

Positioned for Promise

My journey through process, has been both painful and prosperous. God has done some amazing things. I never would have believed if I did not see with my own eyes. God promised me that I would get out of debt, I am nearly financially-free. God promised He would save my family, everyone in my household is now saved. Salvation, healing, deliverance, and miracles are visiting my extended family! Incredible God! God promised that for my shame I would have double (Isaiah 61:7). Some of the things I lost in the process, God has exceeded the double, in some areas, He quadrupled. I was tired of trying to be someone I never was supposed to be. I was tired of trying to make sure people were comfortable around me, careful not to offend even when it came to God. Finally, I am who God has called me to be, unapologetically.

I am delivered from the opinions of others. I used to live a life of fear: fear of rejection, failure, loss, fear of not adding up and fear of succeeding. I lived in fear for so many years. My biggest fear was that people would reject me if I totally obeyed God's call on my life. You know what? They did. But I became fearless! Well, through process, I am triumphing. I learned that if I speak God's word in truth and love, the rejection is not directed at me, but God. I learned if I lose anything doing the work of the kingdom, I gain. I gain in this life and eternity (Mark 10:29-31). If I fail by man's standard, it means nothing, I am not of this world. I am so grateful to be chosen by God.

I rest in knowing that I am not required to live up to the expectations of the world. Through process, I learned that I am fearfully and wonderfully made, God ordained me before I was in my mother's womb. God has given me love, power, and a sound mind. He is awesome. He prepared a place where the unique gifts and talents He blessed me with are accepted and people's lives are changed. I no longer live in fear of God's judgment. I realized that traditions of men crumble in the presence of Almighty God. Spiritual bondage is not the will of God for His children. "Whom the Son sets free, is free indeed." I am so incredibly grateful for the processes that God has taken me through. I know who I am. I know who God is and why He saved me. Praise God, I rest in grace.

These processes have been about gaining the ultimate promise and prize, Jesus. The Promised Land is walking in the will of God without fear and resting in the promises of God's word. I learned that nothing I do warrants God's blessings. I used to think if I made a bad decision it would cost me eternity, God delivered me from salvation by works. Nothing we do can save us. Our works do not save us, we are saved by grace lest any man should boast (Ephesians 2:8-9). I can love unconditionally, I am able to love my enemies, bless them that curse me and pray for them that despitefully use me. Being in a room with people who despise me, used to eat at the core of my being. I can love them without expecting anything in return. Growth has happened. I am no longer a prisoner of emotional baggage from anyone not even my own. I am only a prisoner of the Highest God.

With conviction I can tell you, God has the best plan for your life. He has some tough requirements, but they are for your good. God never leaves us hanging. Until we lose everything, we will never know God is enough. Until we are shattered, we will never know how awesome God has made us. God and His will are all that matters. When God allows extenuating circumstances in your life, it is to bless you, not destroy you. God promises that after you have suffered awhile, He will establish you and make you perfect. After you have done the will of God and patience has her perfect work, you **will** obtain the promise. I am not sure what God has promised you, but obey Him fully, forgive Him for what He allows or what He does not change. God can see what you cannot.

Deuteronomy 28:1-13 details all the promises that God grants for our obedience. Imagine being overtaken by blessings. God promises to bless your children and the work of your hands. The

Lord will work wonders with your enemies. God will establish you to himself. The Lord promises to make you plenteous, not experiencing drought but abundance. God will open up his good treasure and the Heavens will torrentially rain in your land. The Lord will make you the head and not the tail, you will be a lender and not a borrower. All of these promises are available. The prerequisite is enduring the *"Pain of the process."*

The purpose that God has for your life is worth all the pain, tears, losses, sickness, disease, setbacks, and persecution that flows from a radically obedient life. Withstand the heat of the inferno, then you can withstand the overflow of blessings. Endure the process, it is worth it! The pain of the process is about conforming to the image of Christ. It is not about receiving the manifold blessings, although they are pretty awesome. The blessings are an added benefit. ***The Power of Process*** changed a fearful, bound, crippled believer into a fearless, free, courageous warrior. I walk in my promise daily. I have not seen everything because I am still living, but I am thankful for the journey.

It is my prayer that God anoints you to endure your process, and that you experience incredible transformation into the image of Jesus.

I am convinced that your latter end will be greater than your beginning. **God bless you!**

ABOUT THE AUTHOR

DR. NIKKI HARRIS

Dr. Nikki Harris is a veteran educator of twenty-four years. She has served as a classroom teacher, department chair, and a member of school administrative teams. She has also served as a college professor and a leader in higher education administration. She trains teachers and administrators on how to educate effectively. She is a graduate of the University of Tennessee at Martin and Union University with a Master of Education. She holds a doctorate in Leadership and Policy Studies with an Emphasis in Servant Leadership. Throughout her professional and ministerial career, she has developed and authored curriculum and training materials, community outreach programs, and grants. She has conducted grant management. She is most grateful for having the opportunity to train and develop leaders. Dr. Harris has appeared on local news shows and Christian television programs, such as the Trinity Broadcasting Network(TBN) as well as hosting her own television program, "Created to Be by His Side," where she featured ministries and businesses of local leading ladies.

She is a prolific writer and speaker with writings published in *Christianity Today*. She is a contributing writer for Urban Ministries, Inc. Dr. Nikki Harris is most noted for her aptitude to handle the Word of God with passion, precision, and poise. She teaches, mentors, and trains women with anointed Bible teaching that transcends culture, age, and religious barriers. She has ministered to young girls through the "Bridge of Hope" and "Precious Jewels" ministries. Through these ministries, she combats the forces of darkness by helping rescue the next generation from the grips of hell. She ministers in her local church, city, and state and has been called to establish ministries for leading ladies in various states across the United States. She has been called upon to minister internationally as well. Recently, Dr. Harris founded Teen$preneur and Girl$preneuer to equip the next generation of entrepreneurial servant leaders.

Dr. Harris ministers alongside her pastor husband, Apostle Brian Donald Harris of Dominion Living Ministries in Memphis, TN. She willingly labors with her husband in training, activating, and releasing laborers for the kingdom harvest. Together, they take pride in teaching God's people to take dominion and live the kingdom life. She is the founder and visionary of "By His Side Ministries," a multicultural, interdenominational, and international ministry vehicle that equips ministry wives to labor in the vineyard with power and anointing alongside their husbands. She believes that a woman married to a man in ministry is anointed by God to help her husband have *Dominion*. In 2014, Dr. Harris, along with her husband and other local clergy leaders, founded "When Pastors Pray," an outreach ministry that helps pastoral and clergy leaders overcome depression, discouragement, and burnout, and addresses the prevention of suicide among clergy leaders.

Dr. Harris recently served as the Chief Executive Officer/President of The National Coalition of Pastors Spouses, which has led the African American church in taking a stand on health education, awareness, and prevention. The National Coalition of Pastors Spouses was founded by the late Lady Vivian Berryhill, who envisioned the church taking back the black community and overcoming diabetes, heart disease, Aids/HIV, teen pregnancy and other health and non-health related challenges that have plagued the African-American community.

To contact Dr. Nikki Harris

DrNikkiSpeaksEnterprises, LLC

2170 Business Center Drive

Memphis, TN 38134

901.679.2023

website: www.drnikkispeaks.enterprises

email address: drnikkispeaks@gmail.com

www.ingramcontent.com/pod-product-compliance
Lightning Source LLC
Chambersburg PA
CBHW030930090426
42737CB00007B/378